PENGUIN BOOKS

DIVORCE IS NORMAL

Born and raised in Chennai, and continuing to grow up in Mumbai, Shasvathi enjoys stringing words together. A divorce changed her life irrevocably, and she takes pride in how she took it in her stride. A fervent advocate since, she battles to destigmatize divorce, envisioning a world where it's embraced and accepted in every household. Her words have found homes in prestigious publications such as *Vogue India*, *Quint*, *Vice India*, and she has graced the TEDx stage as well. Wherever an opportunity arises to dismantle the stigma around divorce, she seizes it, using her voice to promote acceptance and understanding.

T0025977

Celebrating 35 Years of
Penguin Random House India

DIVORCE IS NORMAL

SHASVATHI SIVA

PENGUIN BOOKS

An imprint of Penguin Random House

PENGUIN BOOKS

USA | Canada | UK | Ireland | Australia
New Zealand | India | South Africa | China | Singapore

Penguin Books is part of the Penguin Random House group of companies
whose addresses can be found at global.penguinrandomhouse.com

Published by Penguin Random House India Pvt. Ltd
4th Floor, Capital Tower 1, MG Road,
Gurugram 122 002, Haryana, India

Penguin
Random House
India

First published in Penguin Books by Penguin Random House India 2023

ISBN 9780143454670

Typeset in Adobe Caslon Pro by Manipal Technologies Limited, Manipal

www.penguin.co.in

To my incredible family,
for their unwavering support.

To my beloved dogs,
for their comforting presence.

To my steadfast friends,
for holding me through tough times.

And to my remarkable husband-to-be,
for believing in me wholeheartedly.

Contents

Introduction

Hello, readers!

2019 was a year of rebirth for me. I was newly divorced, and the world felt like a different place. The more people asked me to hush up about this taboo topic, the louder I wanted to scream. As I dug deeper, I sadly began to comprehend the staggering extent of the stigma surrounding divorce, even in today's supposedly progressive society. It was . . . shocking.

Driven by a burning desire for change, I felt I had to do something. I firmly believe that one of the most potent ways to dismantle this stigma is through open conversations, refusing to shy away from the topic.

And so, I embarked on a journey. I harnessed the power of social media to find my voice—a voice that has led me here today, presenting this book to you. Within these pages, I aim to guide you through the labyrinth of divorce stigma as seen through the lens of Indian society.

Moreover, I aspire to instil in you a profound sense of hope—a hope that transcends the boundaries of divorce and shows you the limitless possibilities of a remarkable life beyond.

I invite you to embark on this journey with me. Together, let us challenge preconceptions, inspire change and embrace the beauty of resilience.

Wishing you an empowering reading experience!

'Marriage'

Dramatic climax scenes in movies usually have rain pouring in the background, almost as an accessory. In my story, I did too. Except this was a difficult reality. Sometime in the September of 2017, sheets of rain lashed across the city of Mumbai. The windows of my living room put up a nasty fight against the turbulent winds. I got word that water had entered the ground-floor homes of our building. There was a nasty storm brewing outside.

But there was a much worse storm occupying my attention. One that was brewing inside.

That night, I had decided to end my marriage. I felt much like the clouds in the sky; they first swell up with water slowly, then hold in as much as they can, reaching a point of saturation. But it all gets too heavy—and they burst into rain. Maybe even clouds heave a euphoric sigh of relief when they put their burden down.

The storm inside grew ironically calm as the weather outside mellowed into the silence of the night. At 2 a.m., I plonked myself down on the sofa with a cosy blanket and a hot cup of tea, and tried to write a text. I rewrote it about fifty times, and my fingers nervously toyed with the send button. I finally mustered up the courage to send it.

'It's over. This marriage is not working. I'm sorry.'

For someone who otherwise isn't awake at these ungodly hours, that was the day he decided to not sleep. I got a reply within seconds.

':)'

Say, what? Who replies with a goddamn smiley to this? I was furious with my father and also rather confused. I had no words in response to this. I replied with a '?', and his reply to it truly was my rebirth.

'It's okay, it's going to be all right. Whatever it is, walk out with your head held high.'

At this point, when everything in life seemed to be crumbling, I had many reasons to cry. But I broke down in tears because for the first time in almost two years, I found a modicum of strength to walk out of a relationship. If a text message could mimic a warm and comforting hug, this was it.

The thing is, when you've been faced with an impending decision for an excruciatingly long period of time, it doesn't smack you right in the face. It's not sudden, it's not a shock, it's not an impulse. What it is, in fact, is clarity. It brings you composure and most of all, relief. If the end is near, then a fresh start is just around the corner.

I opened a fresh page in a notebook and wrote, 'I tried. I tried very hard. But this isn't for me. Let's go home.'

What a contrast to September 2015, I thought to myself. A good cry and re-warmed tea later, I stared at the rain outside the window and drowned myself in nostalgia.

Planning a wedding is an uphill task generously sprinkled with disagreements, stress, confusion and whatnot. But what it *also* brings is delirious excitement for the future. The appetite to build a life almost from scratch, this time on your terms. I, for one, enjoyed the months leading up to my wedding. Let's not skip the vanity—choosing a venue, picking out clothes, selecting food options, make-up trials, learning to dance, bringing friends and family together and so much more. But that aside, what truly had me feeling over the moon was planning for what lies ahead after tying the knot. The prospect of building a cosy life, a home that I'd love to come back to from work every day, full of companionship, fun, laughter, love and happiness.

Generations across the globe, across cultures, religions, languages and boundaries have warned us that marriage is hard work. But when we're in love and blinded by the exhilaration of a future we believe we deserve, 'how hard can marriage be?' is not an uncommon thought. When the positives outweigh the negatives, cynicism does not come easy, and I'm not saying it should. But marriage seems like a breezy walk in the park until it starts to rain.

I just wanted to have fun, more than anything else. I was only twenty-four, young and naive. *I'm only going to do this* once *in my life*, I thought to myself so often. I loved getting into the details of my clothes, make-up, return gifts, the food and all the other nitty-gritty. The wedding planned for me was far from standard. From shattering patriarchal norms, such as having only both mothers conduct the wedding, to giving equal participation to widows (my aunts, grandmothers) in the ceremony, to having a fully vegan and pet-friendly wedding, it was an event that set a shining example of how weddings can also be radical, mindful and different. I really couldn't have imagined getting married without having my dogs around either— they were truly the stars of the event. With such interesting storylines for a wedding, of course it was plastered all across media channels, articles, videos and social media posts. It added a lot of tension because it was well known that I was married. I was rejecting interview requests even in 2021 from reporters looking to cover the wedding.

Public or private, once your relationship is known to others, a kind of pressure builds. Any event you go to, you're immediately asked how you are, how your husband is, how your married life is. Everything else comes next.

Having strong roots in Madras and Tamil cinema, I've grown up admiring Mani Ratnam's romance storylines and listening to Rahman's melodious tunes that perfectly brought them to life. I always lived in a romanticized bubble. I had a standard notion in my head that love outweighs it all. The almost constant red in my cheeks at my wedding was not from a blush stick. I was radiating joy. Indeed, I was at my happiest on the day I got married. The smile on my face was the most natural it had been in a long time. Whether I made a pretty bride or not, I wanted to be a really jolly bride. I always thought, and continue to believe, that happiness is the most infectious feeling, and it lights up one's face like nothing else. I thought that's the way to set a precedent for a new life taking shape.

I really embraced the idea of playing the role of a wife. With butterflies fluttering away in my tummy, I walked into a new life, starry-eyed. I had big hopes and huge dreams of what this life would look like. Excel sheets of financial planning, vacations, groceries, weekly menus, house parties, lazy Sundays, little traditions, big moments and a lot of love.

There was a sense of accomplishment. I've done it! I've ticked it off my list! Settled and sorted by twenty-five. A really good girl who's adhered to societal norms of what's to be done by this age. Like I'd finished a puzzle and all the pieces fit perfectly together. But if this really was a puzzle, then I soon learnt I was a piece that didn't belong to this set.

The red blush in my cheeks faded much sooner than I'd expected.

By December 2017, two months after deciding to formally separate, things weren't very different. It was still blurry. Getting married is a big decision, but deciding to end a marriage is an even bigger one. Marriage in its very essence isn't just about two people but about two families coming together. As much as I'd love to paint the town red screaming at the top of my lungs that 'it's *your* choice', there's a lot of other factors that need to be taken into consideration.

My decision was quite a surprise to many who knew me well. For that, I take responsibility. Today, I can write this without attaching shame to it—I presented a false narrative of being extremely happy for a long time. To family, to friends, on social media: that life was everything I'd expected it to be. When reality caught up and the strain of putting up an act hit me hard, I had to cave in and stop lying. Especially to myself. This is why the saying 'you don't know what's happening behind closed doors' is tossed around so often. I could've been smiling on the outside, but it didn't change the reality. Neither did plastering on a fake smile. This is probably more true for women than it is for men—we are put under undue pressure to hold families together. We are expected to be the ones who will rectify problems, put up with bad behaviour, adjust in unjust situations, smile on the outside, no matter what's boiling on the inside.

A decision as big as this takes a while to digest for near and dear ones. It's not easy breaking the news, and it's not easy listening to it either. Among many other questions, one stood out for me as most striking: Why did it take me two years to make this decision? I was asked this repeatedly. My only answer to this is that I wasn't ready. I can tell you this with utmost confidence: until *I* felt ready to face reality, speeding up the process would have exacerbated the problem gravely. In all honesty, this wasn't an acceptable answer to a few.

Let me try to break this down bit by bit. Before announcing a separation, there are certain elements that need clarity in your head. First and foremost, it is extremely important to introspect and come to terms with what *you* want, which is not something somebody else can do for you. It's your decision, and yours alone. This is what I followed. I took a step back from work, family and friends, and tried to befriend my thoughts—thoughts that were warped in a myriad of emotions. I was angry, upset, empty, confused, irritated, relieved, calm and happy all at once. How does one make sense of this? It was crucial for me to accept each of those feelings and work through them. I wrote down my thoughts and let them flow. Calm always follows the storm, right?

I took my time, but once I made peace with wanting to separate, it became somewhat easier to communicate it. Time gave me the space to find answers, reasons and responses. But oh boy, the questions that come your way! As for me, I saw the separation coming for a long time, so I had time to process it. For those who were on the receiving end of this sudden, dramatic change, it wasn't easy. The shock factor took a while to wear off. I was met with rounds of questioning, shock, surprise, confusion and then some more questioning. But isn't it fair? When I spent months mulling over this decision, shouldn't I be kinder to those who've not even had a few days to make sense of this new chaos I've thrown at them? I took deep breaths and tried to navigate through every speed breaker carefully, and turned to my closest friends for comforting hugs and long crying sessions.

My favourite character of all time, Lorelai Gilmore said, 'Little by little it's getting easier to pretend it's easier, which means easier must be right around the corner.' She was right. And I promise you, it will get easier for you too.

The tricky part, however, remains that these feelings are a constant ebb and flow. One day you wake up feeling like all's right with the world, and the very next day you cannot understand why the weeping refuses to stop. It gently topples over you in waves. Sometimes, it attacks you when you least expect it. I remember once staring at an ice cube tray and not understanding why it was causing me immense pain. That feeling of doom used to begin at the very core of my stomach, the flux of anxiety rising to my chest, tightening and strangling my breath, where I would try to swallow it and make it go away, but it was stubborn and soon reached my eyes, and the waterworks would begin.

While I tried to process more of my thoughts, past trauma and the immense pain I was feeling, it sort of caught up with life, leaving me less confident, unsure, timid and terrified of the world that suddenly seemed big and bad. It took time and hard work for the frequency of anxiety episodes to gradually reduce.

A question I had to answer not just once, but pretty frequently was 'but why didn't you tell me before?', particularly from my mother.

It took a lot to compose myself and give meaningful answers. I realized while talking to someone very close to me who also went through a divorce that she felt the same way. It's not an uncommon question, and neither is it uncommon to skip a beat before answering this. I often just wanted to say it was 'my wish', but it's not as easy as that, is it? The truth is, I needed time to process. Until I was ready to tell someone, nobody could have taken it out of me. It took a long time and a lot of effort for me to extract the guilt associated with this question. I was in no way obligated to share it before I wanted to. Some people can process difficult situations rather quickly, and some can take years. For me, it was a challenging journey of perseverance.

I changed my answer to make it more sensitive and approached it with more patience, including the tone in which I communicated it. I think it's important to be cognizant of the fact that not everybody will respond calmly to your issues, even if you are calm. The minute it's whispered into another's ears, it's your added responsibility to ensure that it doesn't spiral out of control. This holds true all the more for one's parents, mostly out of love and concern. The one thought I kept going back to was, 'If I was old enough to be married, surely I'm old enough to deal with everything that comes with it.' But of course, it took work on my part to understand that it could be shocking to my loved ones, and I needed to give them the time to help them grapple with it.

But this is my story, and I shall narrate it the way I choose to.

Basking in this acceptance was the balm I needed to begin healing. Let me also tell you the advantages of taking your own time. It gives you the space and bandwidth to arrive at a decision that isn't hasty or influenced by others. I got to sit with my feelings in silence, to arrive at a conclusive decision that I was convinced of. I also had the space to try and hunt down an answer to every possible question that I could think of. If I showed conviction in the way I spoke about this difficult decision, then there was little left to chance.

Having said that, I won't lie. *None of this* is a cakewalk. Like I said, a marriage is never just about two individuals, it's always about two families. Many a time, even if it's the two individuals who are the most affected by a split, the onus of ensuring the rest of the family's acceptance will also fall on the couple.

I speak from experience when I say this: my biggest superpower in that moment was the patience that allowed me to take ample time to come to terms with a marriage that wasn't working. I continue to wear this as a badge of honour. Patience isn't easy, but I'm so glad I found the strength to hold on.

And while I could gloat about that to the moon and back, there was something humongous staring me in the face that I couldn't even begin to think about:

Divorce. Yes, with a capital D.

'Divorce'

This word is usually pronounced two different ways: dIvorce or diVorce. Regardless of how it's pronounced, what a scary, heavy word. I had begun to make peace with the separation, but divorce? No way. It was too big a deal. Very close to when I decided to separate, a friend casually asked me, 'So, when will your divorce be done?' My heart stopped in its tracks. I couldn't wrap my head around it at all. I felt triggered, attacked and extremely ashamed. I told her I didn't know, and to not ask me about it. For days together, I couldn't stop thinking about the question and what it did to the very core of my existence. As I had tried to deal with the separation, I tried to apply the same formula in the new situation I found myself in: one step at a time.

This time around, these were the smallest steps ever taken. The first step was to ban the word divorce among my friends and family until I felt ready to utter it. If we *had* to, we'd say 'D'. Everybody obliged. If this had to happen, it was going to be on my terms.

I felt cheated by the power of the universe. I'd stare at the ceiling for hours wondering why this was happening to me. I had walked into something that I thought was forever. Did I dream too much? Are others also living this way and not saying anything? Am I that naive and stupid? Questions to which I couldn't find answers, and never will.

I was also surprised at how much internalized stigma existed in my system. How did this creep in? Did I have passive thoughts about it? I don't think I ever did. As a matter of fact, I had never given the word divorce any consideration in my life. All I knew about divorce were things I'd picked up subconsciously from others, very loosely.

Having a set of really close friends is the biggest support I could ask for. It's a privilege I never take for granted. This period of time taught me a lot of things, and one of them would definitely be that the friends who stood by me through this ordeal are the ones who love me most fiercely. It took a lot of patience to deal with me as I went through this. I heard much later from one of my closest friends that they had to 'walk on eggshells' around me at times, and I cannot imagine how many days that went on for. These were my people and my cheerleaders. You cannot imagine how often these small and big gestures from supportive friends can have a lasting effect on your life.

Living through something as intense as a separation or divorce also means it's a make-or-break situation for many others: friends, family, colleagues, etc. I definitely felt my friend circle quietly close in. I was on guard about who I talked to and how much I shared. Some understood, some didn't. Those who did, sat through midnight howling sessions, angry voice notes, unreasonable mood swings and complete doom. I remember an incident at 3.30 a.m. one morning when I couldn't sleep. I shared with a friend in complete anger, 'I hate the world, I hate everything, I hate everybody.' She dutifully replied with what I really wanted to hear then, which was that the world sucks. She made a joke or two, and also ended up sending me ice cream the next day. Having gone through this with my friends, I can confidently say that we've built a bond for a long time to come. As I sat down to speak to many others about their experiences with divorce, I found that this was common— how we relied on friends to get through our worst days. In particular, I loved Shruthi's story of how her friends surprised her with a getaway in between two court dates and whisked her away for a week to help her feel better. It's the little and the big things put together that make it easier to stay afloat.

* * *

December 2017 was coming to a rough end, and my parents wanted some sense of where I was heading. I didn't have answers, and the best I could come up with was a deadline. My best friend was getting married in February 2018, which gave me two whole months to work things out. I wanted to focus on helping her through the wedding and decided to use that time to help myself inch closer to accepting the 'D' word. It was the ideal cut-off point. Two months. Fair game.

This particular wedding also showed me how deeply my friends care for me, and their actions spoke louder than words. My best friend's wedding was extremely important to me. I was attending the wedding without a plus-one, which means people were likely to ask, 'Oh, how's your husband?' 'Where's your husband?' 'All good? How come your husband isn't here?'

I was dreading it. I hadn't mentioned this to my friend. This was her day, after all, and I didn't want to be a damp squib. The festivities kicked off with pomp and happiness, and to my pleasant surprise, nobody asked me a single question. Here's a family I've known for many years, other friends and acquaintances who I'm familiar with—and not a single question. Two days into this, I became curious. I took the bride aside and asked her to quickly sum up in thirty seconds how this was happening. With a sheepish smile, she told me that she'd informed her family, friends and everybody she could get a hold of to not check in with me about this in particular. Other friends were put on duty to ensure this practice continued. How diligently it was followed!

I felt safe and protected. I heaved a sigh of relief and loosened my shoulders, knowing I could enjoy this event without having to hide in fear. I can never forget what a relief it was to not be on the receiving end of prying questions. I'm fairly certain there was talk behind my back but that's beyond my control. What meant the most to me was how my friends drew a figurative wall around me and didn't let anybody enter this palace of peace. It takes effort to do this for someone else, and if you ever find an opportunity to protect someone you love, kindly go ahead and show them your shining armour.

My thoughts about divorce were almost amusing to me. Where is this stigma coming from? Who told me that divorce is something to feel guilty about? When did I become this person who caved in to what society thinks? So. Many. Questions!

Somewhere along the way, Indian society has villainized divorce and conditioned us to think about it in a certain way. This is rather appalling only when you think deeply about it, or it hits too close to home. Until that happens, maybe you've not given the concept of divorce, or the consequences of one, much thought. The scariest part of a divorce for me was the fact that it was so permanent. Once you're divorced, you're divorced forever. Was that a tag I was willing to live with? Maybe not. But what choice did I have?

The weight of these thoughts was dragging me down in so many ways, and I was sinking. The forces were too strong with this one.

What about dating? Would a man look at me for who I am, or would the fact that I'm divorced be a barrier? Did this mean I would only be able to date/marry a divorced man again? If I dated again, would it make me look 'easy'?

How did single, never-been-married-before, men look at divorced women? Where did I stand on the eligibility scale now? Would they proceed with caution? A divorcee wants to live her life as a free bird. Is that even possible?

The Divorcee Tag

Now, let's come to the word 'divorcee'. That's quite a tag. I find this extremely problematic for many reasons. Society has reached a point where you're permanently marked if you make the godforsaken choice of walking out of a marriage that didn't work for you. You're stamped and branded, whether you like it or not. Think about this and think about it profoundly. 'Divorcee' defines you by your past, whereas 'married' or 'single' defines your present. Present status is acceptable, why, even understandable, but why does my identity need to be tied to the past? Yes, I got a divorce. But I don't need it to be a part of me as I continue with so many other avenues of life. When I'm single, I'm referred to as single, not what I'm not. Define me by my current status, not by my past.

The stigma associated with a divorce runs so deep that we're called divorcees so we never forget that we made a choice society doesn't approve of, even if it's entirely legal to do so. It's placed in congruence to who you are, who you want to become and what you want to do.

From government forms to visa applications and so much more, this branding continues. I urge you, my fellow readers, if you're divorced, to call this out when it isn't necessary. To question others when they call you a divorcee. To stand up for being addressed by your current status.

I refuse with every atom of my body to be called a divorcee.

Accepting a Divorce

I was merely twenty-seven, and none of my friends seemed to be going through anything remotely close to this. I felt isolated. I'd dive into self-pity sometimes and wonder if others looked at my plight and felt relieved that it wasn't them. I almost felt ashamed that a decision I took with so much pride and joy came to such an unexpected conclusion. I felt like a failure, having wasted most of my precious twenties.

Someone casually mentioned to me, 'What's the big deal? It's just like a break-up. Get over it!' I didn't know how to react then, and the more I thought about it, the more incensed I became. How is it the same? There is no refuting that break-ups can hurt and cause immense trauma, but divorce is a whole different ball game. A marriage brings two entire families into the picture. A truckload of opinions, emotions and baggage come along with it, making this a highly complex process to go through. The couple, apart from facing their own pain, also ends up dealing with the hurt those around them are going through. I've experienced and seen enough break-ups around me to know for sure it is not the same. No offence to the person who said this to me; it was well intentioned. But the difference became apparent to me only when I started to dig deeper. A break-up is the beginning of a divorce, but it doesn't end there.

So many thoughts are swirling around in my head as I try to slowly make sense of it. Like tangled earphones just pulled out of a jeans pocket. It was frustrating to untangle but had to be done. For there is good music at the end of the chore.

Let's go plunging into the past once again. The two months to February 2018 seemed to be closing in on me rather fast. I was struggling, trying to come to terms with the impending doom. One day, after several months, I decided to open Twitter. I wasn't even sure why. But here's where I'm convinced the universe was looking out for me. In the first couple of tweets I read, there was one that said something along the lines of how a divorce was the best thing that happened to her. I was astounded. How was this the first thing I saw when I opened this app after a long break? I stared at it for a few seconds in disbelief. Instinctively, I DM-ed her asking for help.

The incredibly kind, beautiful person she is, Sarita immediately responded. She was more than willing to help me out.

'I'd love to meet you for coffee, but I live really far away. In Navi Mumbai.'

'Oh! Guess what? I'm only fifteen minutes away. I also live here.'

'Great! Coffee?'

'Y E S.'

Coincidences kept building up. That was one coffee date I'll always be grateful for. It was life-changing.

I sat on one side of the table, a meek, scared, under-confident woman, ready to break down at any point. On the other side was a confident, sassy, bright, happy woman. She once again told me how her divorce changed her and turned her life around. That divorce is not a bad thing, to not listen to society but to own my decisions, and to do what's best for me.

I had possibly heard this before from friends and family, but for the first time I wasn't just listening—I was slowly believing it. That's the power of experience. It's so much more believable when it comes from someone who's been through what you are about to go through. Overwhelmed is not sufficient to describe how I was feeling. No. I was a sponge that was absorbing all that she had to say. A flurry of emotions rushed through me. I felt touched by a ray of hope for the first time. It was a beautiful feeling. One I'll remember forever. When it's a life-changing moment, you just know.

She told me about her marriage and why it didn't work out for her, how it started getting complicated, and how she inched towards wanting a divorce. She described the steps she took, how she approached a lawyer, how she went about her divorce, and how unbelievably freeing and wonderful her life has been since. Unbelievable, indeed. I sat like a doe-eyed deer and watched her talk, soaking in every word and searching for hope in every letter.

The sun felt like a soothing balm on my face when I left the cafe, and I waltzed out with a smile. 'If she can do it, maybe I can too,' I thought.

This sentiment holds true for the support group I set up, a long time after this incident. As humans, we thrive on relatability and comparison. We want to say, 'Oh my God! Yes, me too!' and bond deeply over that feeling. To not feel alone, particularly when the feeling isn't positive, gives us the solace that we have company in our misery. No divorce is easy, or even the same, but knowing that you aren't the only one going through tough times makes it a bit easier.

But here's the deal. By saying this, I don't mean to undermine the support we receive from friends, family and well-wishers. What comes from good intentions is always more than welcome. Even in my case, I heard from quite a few people around me that I'm going to be all right when the divorce ends. I'd smile and thank them honestly, but a lingering, persistent question remained in my head: 'But how do you know for sure?' Call me cynical, but this was the case.

However, when I heard almost the same words from someone who had been in the same boat I was setting sail in, I believed it. Hope is a beautiful thing, especially when it comes when you least expect it. 'If they can do it, I can do it too' is an underrated feeling. I cannot tell you the value it holds. I'm not saying that the fears vanish, or feelings change overnight, but the heavy burden lightens with every step.

Life after that meeting at the cafe changed, albeit slowly. I realized I needed to speak to more such people. I didn't know where to begin looking. I was afraid of the questions I'd be asked. I wanted to listen to others but I didn't want to talk about myself. Was that fair? I didn't know. I couldn't tell.

It's true. When you start looking for something intently, you end up finding it. Or it ends up finding you. One way or another, I found more people to talk to. People who were friends of friends, acquaintances, strangers. They were kind enough to open their hearts and doors to me and expect nothing in return. I cried to them, laughed with them, drew inspiration and found motivation. I chipped away at the walls I'd built around myself.

I'd like to think I'm a person who never cared much about what other people thought or what 'society' expected of me. But I found myself caught in a situation thinking thoughts I've never encountered before. My father rebelled against a lot of traditional practices and views, so I grew up in a fairly progressive household that gave me ample space to question accepted norms and make my own choices. But even with that privilege, I cannot pinpoint why I felt this emptiness inside when I thought of a divorce.

Reshma said this as she broke into a dry laugh, 'Oh, I was terrified!' and then followed it up with, 'but what had to be done needed to be. Saying the word divorce out loud brought so many reactions. The sad part is that I needed to handle every single one of them whether I liked it or not.' In contrast to that experience, Sheeba said she was completely ready for a divorce. How refreshing that was to hear! Sheeba was in an unhappy marriage and knew she was wasting her time. But to her advantage, her ex-husband thought so as well. They decided to part as friends, sign divorce papers, and even go out for a drink together to celebrate a new life. This also shows how different our individual experiences are.

I wasn't afraid of what people would think, but I was worried I'd have to explain myself repeatedly. I was concerned my parents' style of parenting might be questioned. There is also a lot of judgement attached to 'love marriages' versus 'arranged marriages'. Would people focus on the fact that I chose my partner as opposed to my parents choosing one? Could someone come up to my father and say that this collapsed because we didn't conduct a traditional Hindu wedding? Maybe my friends would tell me I was too young to make this decision and hence I found myself in the soup? It's possible that people would think I was too weak. Would future partners and their families think I'm too high maintenance?

The issue is that this is a never-ending series of thoughts that doesn't yield any results. Instead, it becomes a huge hurdle to acceptance. People are always going to have opinions in every situation. That is beyond our control. Living my life, whatever little time I've been given on Earth, to the fullest and happiest, slowly started to take centre stage on my priority list. A friend told me something that made me chuckle. 'You, my love, start giving attention only to what *you* think. That, in itself, is so many thoughts. Don't stress your brain with more than that. It will rot.'

I wasn't able to use social media as a means to escape either. I didn't even feel like looking at my profile, full of photos from my married life. I wanted closure and to move on. I mustered up the courage to get rid of it. But just looking at all the pictures laden with memories felt like a huge task. I cannot tell you how important a support system is, particularly in situations like these. I told a dear friend of mine that I wanted to cleanse Instagram. She didn't even let me finish the sentence before she offered to do it. I gave her my password and all she said was, 'Log back into your account when I tell you to.' I felt so protected. The next day she sent me a text saying, 'It's done.' I logged back in and it felt so light and refreshing. I could get back online and do what everybody else was doing—doom scroll. Fun.

On the other hand, Facebook was a heavy load of memories. It couldn't be undone in a day. So, I diligently logged in every day, opened the memories tab and deleted whatever popped up on that day. Three hundred and sixty-five days later, I had done a full purge on my profile. It might seem so irrelevant and small to do this, but the relief you feel at the end of it is something else. As much as we might not fully like it, social media makes up a big part of our everyday lives and personalities. And renewing your account, tailoring it to how you want it to look, can be pivotal in providing the push needed to start life afresh.

Until I wrapped my head around so many of these things, using 'D' instead of divorce worked in so many ways. I think making peace with the word itself is a step in the direction of fighting this fight. Not everybody gets the chance to, though. Payal, for example, lost touch with her husband for a few days following a big fight. She tried desperately to reach him but couldn't get hold of him. One fine day, she was served with divorce papers at her doorstep. She had no time to process the fact that her husband wanted to end things, let alone find the bandwidth to even think of what the consequences of this would be. On the other hand, Prabhu was forced to file a divorce petition on his wife when she refused to have a conversation with him for close to a year and had blocked any contact with him.

Preparing for 'D' was nauseating and scary. There were days with a sliver of hope that I would ride through this smoothly, and there were *many* other days of suffocating anxiety. I'm usually a planner. Even if the plan isn't perfect, I like knowing what I'm stepping into. Here, I had very little clue. I'd done my homework diligently, talking to others, listening to their experiences. But I also knew that mine would be different. I was living, breathing and sleeping through what felt like a nightmare that persisted for months.

It's difficult to end a marriage emotionally, and all the more difficult, legally.

While I continued to try to prepare myself for this task, it wasn't just that I surrounded myself with friends and family who supported me. I also paid attention to the content I was consuming. I was feeling vulnerable and didn't want to watch anything that had an impact on my mental health. Triggers appeared out of nowhere, at the simplest word uttered or a scene watched. Whether it was a joke about divorce, a movie on infidelity, a book about heartbreak, a TV show about single parents or even a post on Instagram about a happy couple, it sometimes hit me in ways I couldn't comprehend. Even a lawyer's robe or a random billboard in town threw me off without much warning. I couldn't visit some cafes I used to frequent, I couldn't drink my favourite juice, and I couldn't listen to a certain band whose music I adored. It was painful, to say the least. On the other hand, Shruthi thought romantic movies from the 1990s kept her hopes from sinking too low. While sharing my experiences with Mythili, she felt the stark opposite. She found comfort in watching horror, dark humour and murder mysteries to keep her company during her divorce. There was some consolation in knowing the world is a very horrible place, she says. We laughed in unison.

I spent a long time trying to answer one question that wouldn't leave my pretty head alone, and later I realized that it's a question that torments so many others as well. 'Why me?'

But here's the thing. How do you find an answer to this? Who would even give me an answer? Nobody. I'd cry into a pillow for hours or stare at the ceiling (believe me, a lot of ceiling staring happened) and wonder if I was the unluckiest person in the world. Obviously, I was not but the mind is melodramatic and enjoys the drama. Clearly, there is no answer to this. I can keep repeating the same question as many times as I like but to no avail. When more important things started piling up, I realized that I didn't have the mental bandwidth to allow this question to torment me and I had to put an end to it. The only way I could stop this thought ravishing my brain was to stop thinking about it. But you know how it goes. The more you tell your stubborn brain to not think of something, the more it thinks of it. The forbidden fruit took the shape of a question. But the more frustrated I got with not knowing the answer to it, the more detached I started getting from the question. I deemed it useless. If the thought still wriggled its way in, I'd just let it pass. Somewhere along the way, after trying too hard and then giving up, which actually was the final solution to forgetting it, I stopped asking that question. Looking back on this today, I'm proud that I managed to shed those unanswerable questions at that difficult time.

Similarly, if you find yourself stuck in this boat without an oar, know that the wind will push you ahead. You're probably never going to find the answer to 'Why me', because things like a heartbreak, separation or divorce don't happen with the level of clarity we might always expect. The sooner you learn to accept that there's no answer, the faster you can move on in life.

Take the wins and learn from the losses.

Stigma: An Ugly Truth

'Take a vacation.'

'Go to marriage counselling.'

'Just give it time.'

'This is very common; every marriage has issues.'

And the best one . . .

'Have a child. Everything will be solved.'

The thing is, free 'advice' is unfortunately readily available. But in so many Indian families, the line between advice and strict orders is woefully blurred. The fear of a divorce occurring in one's family is enough for parents to encourage their daughters to continue living in abusive, toxic, unhappy marriages. They dread her coming back home and the entire family having to face a barrage of rude questions from kith and kin, including but not limited to friends of friends, neighbours, friends of neighbours and families of those friends.

'Over my dead body,' Prakrithi's father told her over the phone. She sobbed as she recounted her story, even though years have passed. 'Please don't come back home alone, there is no place for you here,' her dad then said. She remembered every word, the exact feeling of how it churned her stomach, and the fear it pumped into her system. She couldn't find it in herself for the next two and a half years to leave her husband. The beating continued, and the verbal abuse got worse. 'At least my husband is a good father,' she kept telling herself. But one day, he started to abuse her three-year-old little girl. She walked out, taking her daughter with her, the next day. No family support, very little cash in hand, eyes full of tears and an almost broken limb was all she had. She called up a school friend and asked for a roof over their heads for a few days. A few days turned into a few weeks, and her father cut her off completely. But she learnt to stand up for herself. She procured a well-paid job, asked for help from more friends, found a lawyer who treated her like family and fought a tough divorce case for the next two years.

Her relationship with her parents is still strained. But she wouldn't do it any other way. 'Either they see how happy I am today or they can choose not to. I cannot go back to the abuse I faced from my ex-husband just because they don't approve of a divorce.'

I felt chills listening to her speak! The grit, courage and determination she displayed was admirable. While she managed to get out of this marriage, there are countless others across the country, still struggling. The current divorce rate in India is less than 2 per cent, which is nothing to brag about, as some tend to do, under the illusion that it must mean we have great marriages. The sad truth is that divorce in India is so stigmatized, many don't have the option to leave an unhappy marriage. I imagine this percentage would be much higher if divorce were a socially accepted choice.

Roopa's story truly speaks volumes about how much stigma exists, particularly in smaller cities. Roopa was in love with Satish but due to caste differences, neither family agreed to the relationship. The resistance was more from Roopa's family than his. To stop her from going ahead with this relationship, her family quickly got her married to another man they found via their family circles. Roopa barely had any conversation with the person she was married off to, while being completely heartbroken about Satish. She was shipped off to another country with her husband. In a completely new and foreign land, Roopa was repeatedly beaten, forced to do housework and treated appallingly. Within a few months, she needed to be rescued by the local police, who helped her return to India, to her parents' home. Despite her desperate condition, her parents counselled her to go back to her husband, because the neighbours started asking questions about her return. Thankfully, Roopa stayed strong and held her ground. She refused to go back. After some time, her parents reluctantly started to support her, which was a big step. She managed to conclude her divorce, through a raging pandemic. When she told me her divorce came through, I smiled and thought this was a happy ending. However, she reconnected with Satish after her divorce, and they both realized that the feelings they had for each other never went away. They decided to take the second chance life had gifted them and started a beautiful relationship together. When they wanted to take it to the next level, Roopa faced opposition from Satish's family—this time not because of her caste (apparently, that could have been resolved) but because she's now divorced.

Societal conditioning is also so rigid. It dictates that the man makes the money, while the woman takes care of the house and the children. This may be changing now, but look at how this set-up is skewed against women. So many women put in years of labour—managing a house, cooking, birthing children, raising them and so much more. This prevents them from having a successful career. Financial independence is a major deciding factor for women if they want to leave a marriage that isn't working for them. Unfortunately, even today, there are countless women stuck in unhappy marriages, a lot of them facing abuse, who simply don't have the option of walking out. Where would these women go? How will they find a house? Who will pay the bills? This, in turn, gives men the upper hand, making it easier for them to walk out of a marriage, sometimes solely due to the power of money.

When we speak about societal conditioning, another important factor to take into consideration is the difference between love marriages and arranged ones. The guilt of a divorce in the former can be much higher, and all the more so if there was some opposition before the wedding took place. The couple loses face in front of the family, as their decision to separate is viewed as a failure of what they set out to do. While it is always okay to go back on the decisions you once thought made complete sense, it is difficult for the older generation to grasp that. It snowballs into something much bigger. A therapist mentioned to me during an interview that it's not possible to look at divorce in isolation when it comes to telling one's family about a crumbling marriage. It involves a lot of external factors and relationships that are unique to each family. The relationship between the parents, upbringing, childhood trauma, the level of education, pressure of succeeding in a career and a lot more, could be impactful when a marriage fails.

'My mother went on a three-day hunger strike,' Lokesh said. He and his wife had decided to part ways, owing to a desire for different lifestyles. They cautiously approached his mother over dinner, to tell her of their decision to get divorced. While it was mutual and as cordial as it possibly could be, the family did not make it easy. 'My wife had to bear the brunt of most of it. I remember my mother telling her it was her duty as the woman to adjust to what I want and do whatever it takes to restore the marriage.' He found it downright ridiculous, but logic didn't seem to work. He faced months of blackmail and countless tears from his mother, who still hasn't accepted the decision. He still overhears her on the phone speaking ill of him and his ex-wife for bringing shame to the entire family because of their divorce. Lokesh has mastered the art of ignoring the drama and carrying on with his life, which is currently full of joy otherwise.

Sometimes, a few careless words could be misconstrued and used repeatedly to traumatize someone, as in the case of Zia. Just before her wedding, which was arranged by her parents, her father told her fiancé that Zia could be short-tempered, and in case she happens to fight, to please forgive her and accept her shortcomings. When her marriage went down the drain in less than three months because of a lack of physical intimacy, her husband constantly reminded her of how her father had warned him about her short-tempered nature. It didn't stop there; she was also openly called ugly and blamed for her husband's inability to perform sexually. While her parents were supportive once they came to know of their daughter's struggles, it still wasn't easy for Zia to deal with the situation.

'He flung a glass of juice in my face and threatened violence,' Drishti shuddered when she recounted the incident. Being the only child to a single mother, she put up with the abuse, fearing that society might judge her mother if she didn't. But everybody reaches a threshold eventually. She found a way out and also got her mother's support in stepping out of the marriage. She is safe, happy and healthy today, but it took a long while for her to get there because of the fear of stigma.

Internalization of social stigma is rampant and common for many women. Whether or not we've heard any derogatory comments, there is so much fear that someone might say something that could be hurtful. 'But what if they do or say something' is a thought that crosses women's minds very often, and we're mostly left tongue-tied. A bigger chunk of the overthinking goes into how parents will deal with it. In most cases, relatives, neighbours or acquaintances speak to the parents, and this leads to the spread of the infectious stigma. The onus then shifts on to the parents to handle the pressure of what others say, answer their concerns and stay strong in their support. A generation apart from us, most parents find it hard to stave off this pressure. It becomes a thing of shame—they stop attending social events in the fear of being asked about their child. They don't interact with extended family like they used to. They change their entire way of being. All this because stigma proliferates through our circles faster than light. If only we could have a vaccine against this!

Someone from my family once told my mother about a fifty-year-old man who wasn't able to find a suitable bride, and how they've looked north to south of the country for a 'good girl' but in vain. But now, they are 'even willing to look at divorcees', since there's no other choice. Once you're divorced, you're automatically at the bottom of the barrel where dating and marriage are concerned. It's more of an issue for women than men, for sure. Divorced women are seen as 'easy to get' and frivolous. Divorced men get married to women who haven't been married before, while it's much harder for divorced women to do the same. The *Times of India* reports that according to the 2015 census, 'there are three times as many women as men who are currently single after having been in wedlock.

Over 3.2 million of those separated or divorced are women, compared to 1.6 million separated or divorced men. Both among those separated and among the divorced, there are twice as many women as men. This is likely to be because it is much easier for men to remarry in a patriarchal society.'

I'm not saying it's easy for men. I'm only saying it's even harder for women. A divorced woman is so looked down upon that she isn't found suitable for a man until every other unmarried woman has turned him down. If this isn't indicative of stigma, what is? That's the place divorce holds in society. To be seen as eligible again? It doesn't happen as frequently as it should. We're not your first choice, and it's not fair.

Divorced for the second time, Sumesh was telling me what it was like to get married again. The first divorce, which took him a couple of years to heal from, was much messier than the second. He got married a second time to a girl marrying for the first time. 'Was that not an issue for the girl's family?' I asked him. He said it wasn't, because he's well qualified and from the same community. It didn't work out between them later, but the start wasn't rocky. Now, after two divorces, it wouldn't be easy for him to get married again. I asked him about it, but this time around Sumesh isn't interested in trying out marriage for the third time. 'Two is enough. I'll live with myself for the rest of my existence,' he ended this conversation with a big smile.

I also had the chance to speak to a popular artist, Meenakshi (name changed), who went through a divorce in the 1990s. She was just entering the public eye at the time she got married. She married someone her family chose, without taking the time to find out if she'd get along with this person. Eventually, they did not. After a while, they didn't live together. She wanted to give her art everything she had and her marriage was holding her back. So she decided to end things legally and focus on her very promising career. Stigma, with fame, is a whole different game. The '90s were also a very different time compared to now. There was even less tolerance back then. She was worried about what this would mean for her in her industry—would people look at her differently? Would she lose opportunities, and would she be labelled? She didn't take too much time to overthink this, because even a small lapse in the beginning of her career could cost her a lot. 'I'll figure it out,' was her motto, and that's what she did. Her family, friends and colleagues were supportive of her decision, which made it far easier for her to get divorced. She's always kept her personal life away from the public eye and ensured her art form basked in the limelight. She kept stigma at bay and continues to do so, while being widely successful and incredibly good at her chosen profession.

'Divorces have become common today because people don't want to put enough effort into relationships any more,' a divorced acquaintance said to me. I disagreed with him, quite ardently. Who are we to decide how much effort someone puts into a relationship that isn't ours? Even if someone wants to quit at the first sign of trouble, who are we to judge them for it? This is a prime example of stigma. Once you're married, you're expected to keep trying until all possibilities have been exhausted. Divorce is seen only as a last resort. Why? Effort might feel different to different people. How does one quantify effort? Our bandwidths vary, our tolerance levels vary and our relationships vary. Then where does this comparison creep in? I know of women who couldn't tolerate their spouse for even two months, and I also know of women who put up with their spouses for over twenty years before divorcing them. How can we compare the two? Privilege has a big role here. For some, effort becomes a necessity because they don't have the support system they need to leave a relationship.

A lawyer I interviewed also casually mentioned that in today's world, divorces are gaining popularity because couples aren't willing to make the 'effort'. I shared this online, and it raked up a storm of opinions, all of which gave me deeper insights into what people around me are thinking. In my opinion, to say that today, couples don't put in effort because it's 'okay' to divorce is extremely unfair and judgemental. Every marriage is unique. It's taken many years for women to find the agency and financial freedom to walk out of marriages that aren't working. Divorce is already a heavily stigmatized concept. By adding a layer of judgement to this by putting emphasis on 'effort', aren't we just adding more fuel to the fire? Does someone who does not want to put effort into a relationship need to be shamed for it? Does that person not have the same right to end a marriage? It's taken generations of women's silent suffering for us to find this voice today, so that we can openly take these decisions and speak about them.

After hearing this statement about effort, I continued to ask whoever I spoke to about this topic and their take on it. This was an interesting angle for me to explore as well. Two individuals enter a marriage. What works and doesn't work for them can only be decided by the two of them. More than anything, it's none of our business to evaluate how they've performed in their relationship. Marriage isn't about getting a progress report card. It takes the shape and form that the couple chooses as they sculpt it.

Effort is subjective, suffering is optional.

If a couple decides to end their marriage, let them. If you cannot support this, at least don't stand in their way. Manisha, for example, got a divorce after twenty-two years in an abusive marriage, exacerbated by alcohol, only because she didn't have financial freedom. Twenty-two years of living with a man she didn't care to be with, but she had no choice. She had nowhere to go, nothing else to do, solely because she lacked financial independence.

One of the leading causes for women to continue in unhappy marriages is the lack of funds. It's not rocket science to understand that without money, there's very little room for independence. Being financially dependent on one's spouse can mean losing control, which can severely crush one's confidence. While financial freedom is a world in and of itself, there's also so much family pressure to think about. Where does this family pressure erupt from? Stigma. Parents tell their kids, mainly daughters, to not come back home after breaking a marriage. The pressure is even more intense if children are involved. If they do come back, then what will they tell neighbours and relatives? How will they answer them? As long as divorce is seen as an embarrassment and not something that actually helps people, it will never become a normal topic in households. It baffles me that parents would tell their children to stay in an abusive marriage rather than coming back home to safety, just because society will make it difficult. If we as a community kept quiet and didn't ask a hundred questions, pass judgements, spread gossip and talk about it with prejudice, then no, it would not be as big a deal as it is today. What people need instead is support, love, encouragement and the confidence that they can stand on their own two feet.

'Do you think it's easy for a woman to stand in court when everybody is sizing her up? Do you think it's easy for her to live with the tag of a divorcee? Nothing is easy,' Nandini, a therapist, says. Women are reclaiming their confidence. Today, we have more self- esteem than ever before. Her point is that it's wrong to think it's whimsical or easy to call off a marriage.

You would only say there was no effort put into the marriage when you have no idea how much effort goes into getting out of that marriage.

The Extent of Divorce Stigma

'Every relationship has problems, beta,' said Aina's aunt, a few months after her separation. Aina knew better than to react to that. She'd walked out of a very difficult marriage, leaving her belongings and valuables at her absconding husband's house who wasn't responding to her requests for a mutual consent divorce. Eventually, she was forced to send him a legal notice for divorce. 'But I want to be seen and respected!' she told her family. Her mom's unwavering support is what finally saw her through the divorce, despite her relatives constantly reminding her of the stigma associated with a divorce.

I genuinely didn't know the extent of the stigma that exists until I was done with my divorce and started opening up about it on social media. Even with the small population that I was able to reach out to, the stories I heard shook me to my core. The number of stories that are hidden behind closed doors, in silent tears and loud prayers, is an astounding number. If I could talk to just a thousand people, imagine the actual number of people suffering! It baffles me that we've allowed the fear of a divorce and the stigma around it to prevail over our needs of safety and happiness.

Mahathi told me how her divorce made her realize she's breaking generational trauma. Her family might not have been supportive, but she's seen other relatives who stay in highly toxic marriages because they didn't have another option. But she has made the choice for herself. She didn't need to hide scars like her aunt did, or cry in bathrooms like her other aunt, or stick to a marriage for the children's sake, like her uncle. Hailing from a big family gave her different perspectives, and she's completely at peace with the idea that she's breaking the chain and setting an example for others in her family, affirming that it's all right to get a divorce and be happy.

There are also contrasting stories of support, particularly from parents, that make a world of difference. Reshma's parents not only rescued her from another country from a husband who couldn't control his anger, they brought her back to safety, nursed her back to health and helped her regain control over her life. They, along with her sister, even went to court with her every single time to ensure she never felt alone. 'I realized the stigma was mostly in my head,' she said. 'I postponed my divorce because I thought I'll have to wait for my sister to get married and that his behaviour will actually change by that time, and we could avoid a divorce,' she added. But that's hardly ever the case, and Reshma is sure that she should have focused on herself and gotten out much faster. Her family has bounced back from this incident as a cohesive unit, and she's currently healing extremely well.

'Because I'm a woman and brought up the idea of divorce, I was extremely judged, shamed and scolded.' Supriya married the guy her parents picked and agreed to the wedding when she barely knew him. Now, when she looks back, she sarcastically mocks her decision. She and her husband had no intimacy and barely any communication from day one of their marriage. 'It was an arranged marriage and I thought it'd take time to get comfortable,' was her initial reasoning. But two years later, she found they were in the same sad boat, with no effort or progress from either side. She waited for him to initiate a conversation about divorce, and he did the same. Neither wanted to be the bad person, but how long would they wait for someone to take the initiative? Supriya felt she'd had enough and wouldn't mind being the bad person. Somebody had to step up, after all. Supriya's conservative family were shocked by her decision. While her husband kept quiet, all the blame was put on Supriya for not trying hard enough. This put a lot of undue pressure on her to get out of the relationship while also dealing with the guilt trip others were putting her through. Both families hadn't experienced a divorce before, and this was a big taboo they weren't able to accept. When counselling failed to reconcile the couple's differences, the families agreed to a divorce but very reluctantly.

On the other hand, Tisha's family was incredibly supportive of her amicable divorce. In fact, she and her ex-husband exchanged brownies before the final hearing and continue to keep in touch. But she faced stigma in a very unusual place, and that's when the gravity of it truly hit home. She engaged frequently on a WhatsApp group consisting of feminist-identifying folks, who shared opinions on a variety of topics. One fine day, the topic brought up was whether divorced people need to disclose their status on a dating app bio. Tisha happened to think they don't need to, because it isn't necessary. She will choose to disclose this to people she feels comfortable with, at her own pace. This opinion was met with a shocking 'but it is misleading to not know about this before swiping on someone'. The opinion itself, and more so coming from a so-called feminist group, caught her off guard, and she realized that sometimes we don't even realize how profound the stigma is.

Empathizing with these stories, listening to people and women in particular, made me realize that somebody somewhere needs to begin the process of shattering this stigma. If that means a few more can step out of marriages that aren't working, that's a win I'll take. The effective way to break down stigma is to have open conversations and encourage others to do the same as well.

Tahira's divorce was smooth because of her parents' and siblings' unconditional support. She returned home after three short months, and while her mother had concerns, her father put a roof over her head without any questions asked. She doubted her decision even while she was signing the papers at the court but soon came to accept it. She was surprised that when she opened up to her childhood friends, with whom she'd gone to the same school and college in a small town in Gujarat, she didn't find the support she was looking for. 'This is what marriage is,' said her best friend, and walked away. She never checked in and never bothered to keep in touch after hearing about Tahira's decision to separate. If that wasn't enough, rumours spread among her other friends saying that as an independent woman, Tahira no longer cared for family values. As heartbreaking as it was for Tahira to watch her husband cheat on her, losing her alleged lifelong friends to this ordeal was just as tough. I was surprised to hear this as well. I'd heard umpteen stories of families disowning their kids after a divorce, but this was the first time I heard about one's peers doing this. I was stumped. Luckily, Tahira, who didn't give up the hope and love in her heart, made new friends who continue to evolve with her and support her in a way that's respectful of her choices.

She suffered from stigma at the hands of her family too, albeit a little later. Post her divorce, while Tahira was living her best life, trying new things that she never thought she would, her family started groom-hunting for her younger sister. What would the family think if the elder sister was divorced? Her mother was worried sick. She even asked Tahira if she'd be open to getting married again, which might make things easier for her sister. It was her father who intervened and called it a benchmark for the family that his second daughter would marry into. 'If the family cannot make peace with my first daughter's divorce, I have no reason to get my other girl married into such a family,' he said, thereby raising the bar for both his daughters—their identity and respect intact.

'I was just unhappy, we'd grown apart, and for no other reason,' Anne said about her divorce. 'But is that even a good enough reason to walk out? I mean, he wasn't beating me, or anything. He's a decent man. I have so much to be thankful for, so should I have even considered a divorce?' After a lot of thinking, she went ahead with the divorce and continued to stay in touch with her ex-husband.

Anne's story instantly sparked a thought in my head. Imagine how ingrained the stigma is, if you don't think it's viable to get out of a marriage that's not making you happy because somewhere we believe that only abuse, or something worse, warrants a divorce. What's the reason to break a marriage otherwise? Does only abuse justify a divorce? You might have married someone at a time when it was a decision that fit your life, but it needn't be for life. A few years later, there shouldn't be this undue pressure of being together just for the sake of a legal paper and not because the two people in the relationship want to make it work. Aren't people allowed to grow apart? Aren't people allowed to think and evolve differently, and change their likes and dislikes? Theirs might not be the same as yours, and that's okay! A stagnant marriage can easily turn sour if it isn't given immediate attention. If the losses outweigh the gains, if a future without your partner looks brighter than with them, then it's time to rethink your decisions. I'm not saying every hurdle needs to be met with a divorce. Of course not. Marriage is tough, and it requires constant hard work. It all boils down to how much one wants to give to the marriage, regularly. Yet another reason why divorce needs to be normalized is to remove the stigma from such situations. I sensed the guilt in her voice and face when she told me she had to choose a divorce even though she wasn't abused. Why? Anne and her ex-husband grew apart and had different interests. Why does that mean that Anne, or any other woman or man in her place, does not feel entitled to apply for a divorce?

Prathi and her ex-husband called it quits because after five years of marriage, he started feeling the urge to become a father, while she didn't want to mother a child. Despite being in agreement for four years, their interests in life took an unexpected turn. Neither of them could find a solution to this and hence they decided to amicably split. Today, her ex-husband has become a father, and Prathi has moved to another country where she is laying the building blocks for her entrepreneurial journey. Of course, there was some hurt at the time of the divorce, but eventually they've come to realize they're far better off as friends, showing each other utmost respect. Unfortunately, divorce is still perceived as an extreme step to remedy something that's wrong and not as a healthy option for someone so they can move forward in life. It doesn't necessarily mean that something's wrong. A couple might have grown apart or find they have different goals in life that don't align. A divorce is as normal a decision as it is to marry. If a marriage can last forever, then that's truly a feat. But if it doesn't, we must try to do away with the combined burdens of judgement, guilt and heaviness currently accompanying a divorce.

Latha was expected to be the 'perfect *bahu*' that her mother-in-law deemed fit. She and her husband had to live with their in-laws, in a small town in north India. Latha wasn't allowed to step out of the house alone or work. In hindsight, the family rushed the wedding, which she realizes now is a big red flag. With a controlling mother-in-law constantly breathing down her neck, Latha asked her husband multiple times to help her out in this situation, but she was only met with a 'don't disrespect my mother' retort. Soon enough, Latha found out her husband was cheating on her, and she chose to not keep quiet or put up with his family any more. She managed to reach out to her family to notify them about the goings-on in her marital home. Her parents brought her back home and she wriggled her way out of the marriage through a mutual consent divorce. Married at twenty-two and divorced at twenty-four, a young and bubbly Latha told me how it's so difficult to find a prospective groom after a divorce. She gets profiles of much older men and only men who are divorced or widowed. But not a single proposal like the ones she got when she was looking to marry as a non-divorced woman. I have nothing against divorced or widowed men, but like divorced women, they too deserve to be put in a pool of any unmarried person. 'It's ridiculous!' she squealed and laughed in amusement. 'I don't think I'll even marry again. I'm loving being single. This is too exhausting otherwise.'

The onus of breaking divorce-related stigma does not, I repeat, does not lie solely with the people getting divorced.

Why do I say that? The stigma is all around us. In conversations at your dinner table, in a gossip session about an aunt's friend's brother's daughter getting divorced, with nosy colleagues who can't stop prodding, friends who mock, families you know who cannot find it in themselves to support their own children. It's in your family, your neighbours, people you meet at events, everywhere. I'm fully aware of the fact that it's not always possible to fight everybody's battles; we're all fighting our own at varying levels of intensity. What I mean to say is that marriage is a topic that's broached in every household, which means that divorce should be too. A few words from you challenging someone's stigma-filled thoughts could potentially turn another person's life around. If not, it plants a seed of thought. I've changed, and continue to change the narrative of divorce in my house, with my friends and even at functions. I don't shy away from the fact that I'm divorced. I say it openly. I sit down to speak with those who have questions and comments, to try to have an honest and open conversation about it.

Stigma is everywhere. Sometimes, stigma prevents divorces from happening. Stigma brings with it shame and blame. Let's take Rusha's story as an example. 'A sexless marriage is very common, beta. Have a baby via IVF and your problems will go away,' her gynaecologist said when Rusha tried to explain her marital problems. She lost track of the number of different types of medical professionals she'd consulted to try and figure out the root cause of why her husband could not have intercourse with her. How could having a baby change anything in their marriage? A woman vocalizing her feelings about intimate things like sex has always been viewed through the lens of judgement, and not as something that could be seen as a concern that deserves delicate attention. Like Rusha, so many go through layers of judgement when they choose to talk about issues in their marriage. Rusha's marriage didn't last the test of time. It only became more complicated and unhappy as they couldn't consummate their marriage, thereby putting a great deal of strain on them as a couple. It wasn't easy for her at all, as she was labelled 'desperate'. A divorce, that too because a woman speaks up about the lack of sex in her life, was unacceptable to her family. This was another example of how a dysfunctional marriage can make one feel extremely unhappy, thereby resulting in the marriage breaking down sooner or later.

Little drops of water make a mighty ocean. We all know the value of this saying. Normalizing divorce starts with a conversation about it. A deeply hushed topic coming to the forefront is a start in itself. Divorce as a term is becoming more popular in movies and TV shows as well— sometimes, even as a bad joke forwarded too many times on WhatsApp. It may not always be portrayed in a positive light, but the fact that the word is mentioned is enough to segue into a conversation on the other side of the screen. So, friends, please don't shy away from normalizing it in any situation you encounter. Someone somewhere might thank you some day for that kind gesture.

Watch What You Say

Let's talk about this for a hot minute. It's almost an instant reflex to say sorry the second you hear the word divorce. We're all probably guilty of this. Sure, you might be sorry that a relationship ended. I'm not here to dispute anybody's intentions. A lot of us might have good intentions. But a lot of us also have the wrong words that aren't in congruence with the good intentions. So, I'm here to tell you, please don't say you're sorry without checking if the situation warrants it. The person telling you about their divorce might have gone through years of abuse and has finally found a way to end it. In that case, should you be sorry about the divorce? No. You should be congratulating them.

Every single time someone has said they're sorry when I've mentioned my divorce, I've immediately asked them, 'But why would you be sorry about the best thing that's happened to me?' It's food for thought. Be sorry that the marriage happened but not that the divorce has come through.

As Tisha and I continued to chat, she brought up an important point. She's completely accepted her divorce, and she has no qualms when it comes to telling others about it. But it usually garners an 'oh no, I'm so sorry' reaction. While this might sound harmless, the responsibility of consoling the person hearing this news falls on her. She ends up explaining how it's a normal process, it's a good thing that happened to her, and there's nothing to feel sorry about. It's exhausting to keep listening to the same reaction almost every time.

If we don't encourage such conversations, we also tend to internalize this stigma and let it fester in our system and mind, subconsciously. This is what happened in the case of Yagna. It broke my heart listening to her story. She was brought up with the template of an 'ideal' wife—cooks every meal, takes care of her in-laws, is always there for her husband, and does as they dictate. This is a fully educated double-degree holder, by the way. I'm mentioning this solely as a reminder that unhappy marriages aren't prevalent only in some remote part of the country. It's happening everywhere around us. She did as much as she could, while also trying to balance a career on the side. Between a husband who didn't care enough for her and his parents who put her through so much, she started breaking down. Her friend gave her a reality check, asking her to get out of this toxic relationship, but to Yagna, it was a sacred union in eternity. She couldn't wrap her head around leaving the family.

'Maybe I'm not good enough,' she'd convince herself and get back to the grind, suffering in silence. A sharp slap on her cheek from her father-in-law when she confronted the family about her husband's extra-marital affair really altered her perspective. An emotional slap followed when he said, 'You're so unattractive, why would my son sleep with you?' It was the prompt she needed to walk out because as long as the issues stayed within her house and family, she could handle it. As soon as her husband strayed and cheated on her, she was no longer willing to deal with his dirty laundry. However, a few months down the line, she started to feel the dull throb of the same thoughts again. 'Maybe I wasn't a good enough wife or a good enough daughter-in-law.' Eventually, those thoughts got the better of her, and she returned to her husband and begged him to take her back. She promised him she'd lose weight, cook better, take care of his parents, and whatever else he wanted.

'The best gift I've ever received from him is he not taking me back as his wife,' Yagna beamed. His refusal gave her the new lease of life she needed. While stigma continued to haunt her, she still went ahead and filed for divorce. It felt like the right thing to do. She slipped into a cocoon, unwilling to talk to her friends and family or do anything else. Yagna was always an admirable and accomplished woman who truly didn't deserve what she went through, but with the help of her mother, she is also happy today.

It's easy to be a fly on the wall when you hear others talk about such situations. Some might even consider it gossip, but we're also at a level of awareness where we know these judgemental comments speak volumes about how regressive society still is. Trying to guess the issues between a couple, spreading rumours, always trying to prod and question just to know what happened, is a real headache to the ones going through the actual problems. This is especially true for celebrities, and particularly women who have been on the receiving end of so many assumptions. More recently, influencers can be seen going through the same traumatic cycle as well. The gossip mills keep on grinding. If you're divorced, if you're married, if you're looking to marry or know someone close to you who's married, try and start conversations that might educate others around you. After all, the taboo around a topic only keeps intensifying as the silence around it thickens. One conversation could change a thought or stop the hurt passing on to someone who might be in a tough spot.

Tomorrow, it could be you needing the same support.

This is something I encourage very vocally on social media. Do not shy away from conversations at home, with family near and dear. Speak openly about divorce and its repercussions. After all, education begins at home.

A miscarriage that took a toll on Samara's marriage, along with many other smaller issues which kept adding up, led her and her ex-husband to family court to dissolve their marriage. It took a while for them to reach that stage, with each of them putting different degrees of effort into trying to make it work, but alas, the decision to separate came almost mutually as it reached a point where nothing was working. Samara got married right after college, to someone much older than her. She wishes she'd taken a bit more time to get to know herself better before stepping into a marriage. 'It's been three years since the marriage [ended], and I'm still running around trying to get my name changed back to my maiden name on all documents,' Samara sighed in disbelief. 'Did you know you cannot change your name on a prepaid sim? You can change it only if you convert it into a postpaid plan. And don't even get me started on mutual funds. I've had to send separate emails, documents and signed papers to each and every fund to get my name changed. It's not just that I have to send an email, I also need to pay them to change my name. It's just so emotionally taxing.'

In many cases, even friends end up propagating stigma or hurt without knowing they are doing so. We might say something without thinking it through or without knowing whether it's appropriate or not to say what's on our mind. A few months after Samara's very close friend got married, she asked her how married life was treating her, and mentioned that Samara and her mum had been talking about her. 'I'm extremely well and happy, tell aunty I won't let my marriage break,' came the reply, probably intended in a lighter tone. But statements like these can be rude reminders to those who've made harder decisions in life, like Samara herself. She felt triggered, targeted and small.

Stigma hits in many different ways. Assumptions that someone, especially a woman, is calling the marriage off because she is rebellious or wants alimony, trivialize the complicated, and often harrowing, emotional process of choosing divorce. Concerns over how difficult it is to remarry after a divorce come across as more hurtful than helpful.

I clearly remember an incident where I was made to feel terrible about going through a divorce. For many months after the separation, I didn't open one part of the cupboard where my wedding trousseau was kept. I preferred to ignore it. When I bought sarees for my wedding, I'd ensured that I selected ones that I could wear on other occasions as well. I had no intention of buying something so expensive and heavy that could only be used once. I'd worn these sarees a few times after the wedding, but suddenly, I didn't feel like seeing them again. They were beautiful sarees that didn't deserve to sit inside a cupboard. For many, wedding clothes are full of emotions. Every thread woven into the saree tells a story of the day when your life changed. Brides walk in and out of multiple showrooms to find that item of clothing that would best complement their wedding glow—not just look good on them, but feel good too. In 2019, I'd had enough of seeing my wedding clothing sitting on a shelf. When I finally did look at them, I ran my hands through the pleats of the saree and didn't feel a single emotion. I knew I'd disassociated from them deeply but I still felt I didn't need to keep them. Somewhere deep down, I thought I'd feel better if I parted with them.

I put up posts to sell a couple of my wedding outfits—a saree and a lehenga. I marked them at a much lower price than I'd spent on them, but I really wasn't doing this for the money. A girl, about twenty-six years of age, on the verge of getting married, pinged me on Facebook saying she loved the lehenga and would like to negotiate further. I agreed to a negotiation and we got talking. A few minutes into the conversation, she asked if I had any pictures of me wearing it, and I sent her a link to one of my public photos on Instagram. I guess she went through my profile and realized I'm currently divorced. For the next two days, I didn't hear from her. I nudged her to ask if she was still interested, and she reluctantly told me that her mother was against her buying it, even though she really liked it. Her mother believed that it was *ashagun* (bad omen) and that it might rub off on her daughter. I thanked her for her honesty, and felt miserable, judged and extremely sad. I eventually sold the lehenga, as well as the saree, to someone else.

If you think you want to keep your wedding attire because of the attachment, then hold on to it. You might feel hurt when you see it while you're still in the process of a divorce or while the wounds still feel fresh. Keep it out of sight and forget about it for a while. You never know, your healing journey might soothe the hurt, and one day you can wear those same outfits without feeling any negative emotions.

Many small things, like clothing or jewellery or even a gift, would throw me off guard for a bit. I asked myself so many questions: How did I land up here? What was my future going to look like? Most of all, I started questioning my ability to make any decisions at all. This was the full-blown effect of the stress of everything cascading down on me. I've made many other great choices—my friends, my career, my lifestyle. One unfortunate choice made me question so many things for a brief period and I pity myself for allowing this to happen. It doesn't make me wrong, or even a bad person.

I spoke to Tejasvita, a lawyer-turned-counsellor, and someone who's divorced as well. She had extremely deep insights into this topic from various angles. One thing she said that struck me was that a lot of individuals don't want to be the one to take the final call on divorce. They prefer to wait for the other to make the decision. Why? This itself is the manifestation of stigma in disguise, because it's easier to tell the world that one was forced to leave a marriage, as opposed to saying that a divorce was an active choice. She adds that when it's seen as a choice, it doesn't receive the same treatment as a situation that was thrust upon you. One gets pity, the other gets judgement. It's extremely disturbing that divorce is not widely accepted as just another life choice that someone makes when life takes different turns. The chirpy therapist concludes this from handling multiple cases over the last few years.

Marital roles today have changed dramatically compared to even two decades ago. Today, women and men often have parity in pay cheques, taking seats at boardrooms and working the same hours. So, it's unfair to expect the same division of gender roles. In earlier times, it was clear that the man would go out to work and the woman would take care of the house and the kids. A client

Tejasvita is currently working with is trying to resolve the eternal question of 'who is going to wake up at night when the baby cries' since both parents work the same hours. 'Things are changing today, and rapidly,' she says.

While she had what she calls a 'dream divorce', where it was all extremely amicable and mutual, it was a task for her to get the divorce without vilifying her ex since our law doesn't allow a 'no-fault divorce'. She managed but it wasn't easy. She's currently works as a relationship counsellor with couples in the process of a divorce or those heading towards one.

Is Divorce 'Just a Break-Up'?

I've sat up nights wondering why this is so different from a break-up. Why does society make it so tough to make this decision? We cannot choose the family we're born into but we surely can choose the partner we want to be with. In the event of that choice not working out, can't we be given the choice to move on? Why does it sound like it's not much to ask, but it's made to seem like it is?

Drawing from that experience, I'm going to attempt to break it down into a few pointers on how you can announce your divorce, thereby also breaking the shackles of stigma that weigh you down.

#1: The way you say it

When you say 'good morning' to an acquaintance in a sad tone, they're bound to ask you what's wrong and how you can make it a good morning. However, if you say 'good morning' with a smile on your face, full of happiness and confidence, it might be met with another good morning in return. Similarly, how you tell someone you're divorced, or getting divorced, lies in how you say it. When I say 'someone', I'm referring to someone you don't want unnecessary questions or advice from—the acquaintances you tend to want to stay away from. Trust me, you're not expected to talk about divorce in a positive, happy light. Confuse them. Say it with so much conviction that they have very little to say in return. I've tried and tested it, and it definitely works.

But hey, do not confuse this with toxic positivity. I'm in no way suggesting you need to look happy while feeling low inside. I'm only recommending a tactic I used, that helped me overcome a lot of unwanted attention and advice. It's in no way demeaning what you're feeling, but it can act as a shield to protect you.

#2: Setting boundaries and expectations

Once you've broken the news, you decide how much you want to share. I decided I wasn't letting anybody other than my close family and friends know what I went through. It was an active choice I made. What I experienced was definitely not for public consumption. Anybody who didn't fit into my private and immediate circle didn't need more information. So, when I did tell extended family and secondary friends about the separation, or my divorce, I merely informed them. I didn't divulge details, and I deliberately used text messages to avoid further discussion. I also made it very clear that I didn't wish to entertain questions, opinions or suggestions. Even if it meant I was more curt than usual, I decided this was the path I wanted to tread. Despite this, my mother was subjected to some questioning, but because I had set clear boundaries it was manageable.

#3: Cutting people off

When you are direct with your communication, not everybody will like it. You know what? It doesn't matter. If someone from my external circle chooses to not speak with me as often, it doesn't affect my life. If I have taken the call to cut off someone who managed to sneak in unnecessary questions despite my request not to, then I have no qualms about letting them go. Put yourself first, and you'll see the magic it can do. Proceed with caution and with care.

#4: Exuding confidence (whenever you can)

If you have gone through an unhappy marriage but continued to show the world a fake-happy version of yourself, you'll find this helpful to get through these trying times. You could fake it once, so go ahead and fake it again. Let those who create this stigma be stunned by your confidence. Save your real self for those in your close inner circle. You can break down and share your most vulnerable moments with them. But for those who watch you from the outside, shut them down with your confidence. They thrive on the weak, so show them your strength.

Stigma hurts different people in different ways. Words have a tendency to impact us. They can drastically change how you feel about yourself and send you down a path you don't want to tread. As much as you can, in your capacity, try to shape the narrative so you have control over how people talk to you or treat you. There's no foolproof way considering how intrusive society is, but it's always worth trying.

Try, try, try, till you're free.

Making It Official: Courts and Lawyers

I remember a friend once joking, 'I did get married but never registered it. So, no divorce for me!'

As I spoke to more people, I realized that this is an extremely common misconception that people have. I mean, if only life were that convenient, right?

The absence of a marriage registration does not render your marriage void. You still require a divorce through a competent court to dissolve the marriage. If you've been married as per the customs and traditions of your religion and have consummated your marriage, then you're legally married. So, if you've been married and have not registered it, please don't assume there is no need to dissolve it at the court if you want to separate. You're still required to go to family court.

Every divorce is different, yet so many elements are the same. The content of the papers we hold might differ, but we all still stand in the same building and go through similar legal processes. We face familiar fears, and we deal with emotions that are tearing us apart. I remember standing in court and feeling numb, but I did look around and observe others. The building reeked of panic. The paint was chipping off in dull rooms that lacked fresh air and sunshine, which only added to the urge to leave as quickly as possible. I watched a mother with a young child in her arms cry openly as she held a set of papers in her hand. She was alone, the child too young to understand. I don't know what she was going through, but I hope she's doing better today. I saw another family sit in complete silence. I mean, for an entire day I did not see them utter a single word, other than when the lawyer asked the son a question. I witnessed a full-blown public fight between two lawyers, with their clients standing perplexed behind them. I saw a woman walk out of counselling bawling her eyes out, and a man storming out in anger. I saw the disappointed looks on some parents' faces. Most of all, I saw exhaustion all around me, including my own.

Sitting in court and waiting long hours is excruciating, anxiety-inducing and definitely not something I'd wish upon someone very easily. It was no surprise that every day that I went to court, I returned with the worst headache and fatigue. It felt like I'd done a million jumping jacks in a minute. Almost four years later, I can still feel that in my bones. Walking into court on the very first day was an incident I won't forget. I remember every feeling so vividly.

It took me over an hour to reach the family court in BKC (thanks, Mumbai traffic), and I had no idea what to expect. There was a long queue outside the building before the courts opened at 9 a.m. I stood outside, tightly clutching a file with all the documents I needed. I looked around to get a sense of what others were doing. It seemed like a normal day, somehow. We were ushered in groups of ten into the lift to take us upstairs. I was slated to appear in front of the judge in Court 7, on the third floor. I'd seen so many courts in legal dramas, and I expected the court to resemble them. But it was just a regular-looking room, with a waiting area outside. I was asked to wait there until my name was called out. You remain silent, and do not roam around too far in case you miss your turn. One of the first things I noticed was how the entire courtroom had very little ventilation. I wanted to run out as soon as I stepped in.

I had the good fortune of speaking with a senior advocate and mediator, and former judge of the Punjab and Haryana High Court, Kannan Krishnamoorthy. He had been a student of law since 1974, and we spoke a little about his experience with the law. He mentioned that being able to help other people in situations of conflict has been very fulfilling. I also asked him about how divorce has evolved from earlier times until 2022, and he walked me through a brief history of how it came about.

'Divorce is a matter of personal law. There was no scope for divorce [for Hindus] till the Hindu Marriage Act 1956 was enacted. Christians were governed by the Divorce Act 1869 which was a colonial legislation. Muslim personal law recognizes divorce ever since Shariat was applied in India.

Shariat was a tool of law enforcement when courts were established by the British and had legislative approval since 1937. The dissolution of marriages could take place only through a court intervention, except for Muslims, who could dissolve marriage by pronouncement in writing or orally. Divorce is on fault theory, except when the dissolution is sought on mutual consent. Muslim law does not require any reasons to be given. The recent 2019 legislation called Muslim Women (Protection of Rights on Marriage) Act outlaws the practice of divorce by men on pronouncement of triple talaq.

'It was believed that the bond of marriage was sacred [for Hindus] and it could not be broken. The reformatory zeal that Nehru and Ambedkar displayed had enabled them to push through the legislation despite Rajendra Prasad's intervention. Divorce by mutual consent was through a later amendment in 1976 in Hindu Marriage Act and in 2001 in Indian Divorce Act applicable to Christians.'

He calls marriage a 'complementary arrangement', and advises couples to give space to each other even if their interests don't completely align. He speaks highly of the importance of respect during the course of the relationship, and more so during the time of separation. It might make things simpler, easier and smoother.

When I had to appear in court, I'd reached out to Firoza, a senior divorce lawyer in the family court, Mumbai, for a second opinion and some advice, which was very helpful to me. I recently reached out to her again to speak to her for my book. I asked her what kind of clients she chooses, and whether she turns anyone down. 'I'd fight a divorce, but there are many who don't want a divorce, but just file a case to harass or trouble the other. I can't do retribution. It also adds an immense burden on the courts,' she said, adding that she lays out what can be done in the legal sense, and ultimately, it's up to the client to choose what path they want to tread. It's important that she and the client are aligned in their course of action. She also explained how section 498a has evolved over time. At one point, 498a led to immediate arrest of the husband on the grounds of cruelty, but due to multiple false complaints, the Supreme Court revised it to add that an arrest cannot happen unless a thorough investigation is conducted. While on the one hand, this might help to reduce false cases, it also puts many women's safety at risk. 'The laws might be drafted to enable the woman but the system is that there is no real justice,' Firoza adds. 'We don't have 'no-fault divorce' in this country. Every single divorce case needs to be proved.'

Here's another thing I learnt on my first day at court: that as a woman, my surname gets automatically changed to my husband's name on paper, whether I change it legally or not. Your name doesn't change anywhere else, but it does on the court papers that you file in family court. When I was handed a document, I felt like a tonne of bricks hit me. Did they just change my entire identity? Before I got married, I had decided to use my maiden name for the rest of my life. But here I was, standing in a court of law, being told that this is how it is. I kept staring at my name with the wrong surname, and I felt like I wanted to punch a wall. What choice did I have? None.

I was extremely triggered by this and was told that the bigger issue at hand here was the case itself and that the name barely mattered. However small it might have been to others, I felt extremely diminished and powerless when I saw this. I had to let it go eventually but I doubt I'll ever be able to forget it.

So anyway, I wasn't too thrilled that this was how my first day at court began. I impatiently waited for my name to be called out. Once I marked attendance, we were sent to counselling. I went in alone, explained why I wanted a divorce, and was sent back with another court date two months away. When I came out of the counselling room, I remember asking my lawyer, 'That's it for today?' She laughed and nodded.

Some courts have made counselling mandatory. For example, family court Mumbai, has compulsory counselling. But while talking to many other divorced people, I've learnt that counselling isn't mandatory in other cities like Chennai, Bangalore, Hyderabad, Coimbatore, Surat, etc. It will probably differ case to case, but in Mumbai whoever you are, whatever your story might be, you are sent to the counsellor. When you hear the word counselling, you assume it's something equivalent to therapy—for someone to hear you out and give you solutions. Well, court-mandated counselling isn't exactly that. A counsellor is appointed as the bridge between you and the judge. The counsellor assesses every case by speaking to the couple, and once they are convinced that there is no chance of reconciliation, they produce a 'failure report' that is sent to the judge. If you're really intending to get a divorce, then this might be the one time in your life you'll really look forward to a 'failure'. The judge reviews this and then grants you the divorce, according to their judgment of the case and timelines. Tejasvita asked me this and I fully agree with her, 'Why is it a "failure" if two people don't want to stay in a marriage?' It's totally bizarre that this is what it's called. But hey, if you're going to be stepping into court, I'm just trying to help you to be prepared for what's to come.

The first time I spoke to a lawyer, I was terrified. I find it tough to even describe the kind of emotions that arose in me. I was fairly close to an anxiety attack. I also discovered that your private life is not private any more. Not your sex life, your finances, your chats, your vacations or your family relationships. Everything is now a transaction. For the romantic in me, it was deeply disturbing that even little things that were cute once upon a time, were regarded as 'evidence' now. It truly was heartbreaking to think that it all finally came down to just a document, with the emotions brutally sucked out of it. However, it wasn't the same for my lawyer. She seemed confident that she could wrap this up as promptly. She could see past the emotions, for she only looked at it through her professional lens.

'Are you sure you want a divorce?'

'Yes.'

'Okay, let's get this done.'

A day after meeting with my lawyer, I blanked out. Everything started blurring, and I was sinking in disbelief that this was even happening. I crawled into my bed, unable to move or get up. I wasn't in love, and I wasn't heartbroken per se. It's not that I did not want the marriage to end, but the legalities were so intense and draining that they really took a toll on me.

Talking about legalities, one thing that demands thought and attention is how you collect evidence. A divorce case is a culmination of many things that happen behind closed doors, through spur-of-the-moment conversations and so much more. It's only in a few cases that one is able to record some of this for proof. If you're undergoing some form of abuse and don't know what you can collect as proof, here's where you can begin, as Firoza helps me break it down. Usually at trial, one is cross-examined and you can use the following to corroborate your story. It goes without saying that you should consult your lawyer for your specific case. I'm jotting this down for you to know that there is a way out.

Here's what you can submit as proof.

1. Text messages/voice notes/any form of messaging/ recorded communication with your partner. Even if the fight was at home, it may have continued in messages. Traces of a fight, or even an apology.
2. A confidante: could be a friend, parent, therapist who can turn up as a witness for you. Even if you didn't confide in them, if you know someone who has

witnessed abusive behaviour or seen fights, they can add to your defence.

3. A police complaint filed in the name of the spouse stating abuse can serve as proof in family court.

4. In case of physical violence inflicted on you, a medical report of a full body check-up from a government hospital also helps you build your case.

Do remember that you are under trial only when you file for a contested petition; a mutual consent divorce is far more straightforward and easier to navigate.

For some reason I still can't put a finger on, I found myself sympathizing with Mesha a lot. She too faced similar thoughts in court. We bonded over a number of things and ended up swapping stories as well. Just seven days into her marriage, as she and her husband sat in a quaint cafe in Goa, he broke her heart when he announced with very little guilt that he wanted to be polyamorous. 'Isn't this something couples discuss before getting married?' Mesha asked me, with disgust on her face. Her ex initially even showed her photos of other women and spoke to her about them as if it was the most natural thing for a couple to do seven days into their marriage. He had waited until they were married to let Mesha know about his dual life, since he didn't think she would continue with the wedding plan if she found out before. 'He thought this is the easy way out, that I wouldn't take a decision as big as a divorce, and he could lead his life the way he wished to. He expected to stay married to keep his family happy', Mesha continued.

She joked that her story was worth a movie deal. Month after month, she found more and more women he had had romantic connections with, some even under the pretext of being in an open marriage. She also explained how a lot of Indian men use polyamory as an excuse to cheat and sleep around without the consent of their partner, exactly like in the case of Mesha. She married him thinking it was a monogamous relationship but she'd unknowingly walked into a terrible trap. She was smiling, but her eyes gave away the immense pain she was feeling. I asked her how she finally ended up in court and she laughed before answering. As if she hadn't had enough of living that dreadful life for almost two years, her husband had blatantly slapped a demand for Restitution of Conjugal Rights on her with claims that she was a 'bad wife', 'career driven and money minded', and that she couldn't satisfy him.

In case you didn't know, women cannot be forced to live in their marital home against their will, *even* if legally they're still married. The law protects women and gives us the right to choose where we want to live. For example, in case a husband files a case of restitution on the wife, it's not necessary for the wife to go back to living with the husband. She can very well contest it in court and file for a divorce. Until the case is over, it still doesn't require her to live with the husband. The Constitution protects us all from not having to live where we don't wish to or with whomever we don't wish to.

Mesha was willing to let go of all the terrible things he'd made her undergo with a simple mutual consent divorce, but here he was, tearing her to pieces in court. 'But lies are like worms, they eat their way out of the woodwork in due time,' she says, with a glimmer of hope in her eyes. I reached out to give Mesha a hug, for legalities are not easy.

Preparing for a Divorce

Speaking of legalities, let me take you through how you can plan a divorce. The first thing to know is that you cannot file for a divorce unless you've been legally married (since your wedding date) for at least one year. You're also required to be separated for six months before you can ask for a divorce. I'm noting this down to give a broad sense of what you should know before approaching a lawyer.

There are two ways out:

1. Mutual consent—fairly straightforward. A couple in a marriage want to mutually end it and hence request the court to dissolve the marriage. If the couple decide to part amicably, they can even hire a single lawyer to represent them both and finish it without any complication. They can, however, choose to hire two different lawyers and submit a joint petition as well. There is a six-month waiting period before the court

grants the divorce decree—just in case someone changes their mind. In Covid times, the six months was honed down to as little as two months. There have been more cases when the wait time has been decreased, but six months happens to be the time period for most cases. It's best to check with your lawyer for your jurisdiction.

2. A contested petition—This type of divorce could be a more long-winded process. It's when one partner wants a divorce and the other opposes it. This could take many months or even years to be resolved. There's a Petitioner and a Respondent, and the parties respond to each other via petitions, negotiations and mediators/lawyers. While a mutual consent petition doesn't require one to go into the details of why a marriage needs to be dissolved, a contested petition will need intricate details based on chronology as to why one person feels they want to exit the marriage. The same can be contested by the Respondent. Most contested petitions end up in mutual consent divorces, and that's how the ordeal ends.

To understand legalities, it's highly critical for women to know what the law provides and protects. Women are also protected under the Domestic Violence Act, 2005, so they can feel safe in the comfort of their home. The Act provides civil remedies to victims of domestic violence. It's key to note that the Domestic Violence Act extends to not just physical abuse, but also mental, emotional, sexual, verbal and financial abuse—and that's a very important point because there's a sweeping generalization that domestic violence applies only to physical abuse. In fact, it's termed 'domestic' violence because the cases are mostly when there is a close cohabiting relationship between the offender and the victim. The Act also extends to senior citizens, children, etc., but it is also commonly used to propel a divorce case forward.

According to iPleaders, 'In India domestic violence is governed by the Protection of Women from Domestic Violence Act, 2005 and it is defined under Section 3, which states that any act, commission, omission or conduct of a person harms or injures or endangers the health or safety of an individual whether mentally or physically it amounts to domestic violence. It further includes any harm, harassment or injury caused to an individual or any person related to that individual to meet any unlawful demand would also amount to domestic violence.'

Before you enter into a divorce, it's important to know your rights. This is why meeting a lawyer in advance is crucial. Understanding rights, legal processes, documents and possibilities instils confidence, reassuring us that even though the path ahead might be rough, at least we know what we're going to be dealing with. A lawyer can lay it out for you to understand what lies ahead, how strong your case is, what exactly you need to file, things to expect and so on. The internet might have a lot of confusing sources and technical information that can be overwhelming. I'd recommend you find a good lawyer and set up a meeting to find out more about where you stand. As tempting and easy as it is to open a browser and get lost in pages of information, use the internet wisely so you don't end up feeling confused. Walk into the situation with your eyes open—there's no harm in reaching out and asking for help.

Finding a lawyer can be an intimidating task and I can understand why. I felt it too. I found lawyers quite confident and forthcoming—both of which I was not when I first went to meet them. So clearly, they had the upper hand. Here's an important piece of advice I got from some dear friends—speak to a few lawyers before selecting the one. Also, it's not always necessary for you to pick a very senior lawyer. You can choose a lawyer who might be closer to your age, if that feels more appropriate for sharing intimate or uncomfortable details of your marriage. Deciding who you want to be represented by should be done with care and patience. What's most important is that you feel heard and understood by your lawyer.

I met with a few lawyers, repeated my problem statement and what I wanted, gauged their reaction, and then went with the one I felt most connected with. It's crucial that the lawyer understands your case, your mental state, what you want out of it, finances, family and other related factors. The more at ease you feel with your lawyer, the smoother your proceedings could potentially be. At the very least, it doesn't become yet another problem to deal with.

Shruthi told me her childhood friend was a good lawyer, who recommended a fellow lawyer to work on her case, while her friend assisted all the way through her chaotic contested divorce. On the other hand, Namita mentioned how she found her lawyer online on a list and trusted him to help her. For Tripthi, it so happened that her uncle had a legal firm that did a great job of covering her legal needs.

The best way to find a lawyer is through your social circles. Consulting a lawyer who's worked with someone you know adds a light layer of familiarity, which might aid your comfort. If you are unable to find one in your circle, then I'd recommend checking with support groups. Another way is to look online to see the top-rated lawyers in your city and set up meetings. Legal assistance is fairly easy to find, but do speak to multiple lawyers before zeroing in on one.

I tried a few, and it was easy to gauge their interest from the way they listened to me talk. When I felt comfortable, I eased in and was able to select a lawyer—the one I could rely on to get me out of the mess I'd walked into.

Rashmi switched lawyers in the middle of her trial because she felt a growing sense of discomfort with her lawyer, who constantly passed judgements about her choices. Considering she was fighting a divorce on the grounds of sexual incompatibility, she couldn't speak freely with a lawyer who couldn't understand her. She found another lawyer who validated her feelings and took time to explain what options she had. Today, Rashmi is happily divorced and is extremely grateful that she switched lawyers. She mentioned how doubtful she was of getting a divorce with the first one.

Namita spoke very fondly of how her lawyer was available to her throughout, even helping her through panic attacks and severe anxiety. She dealt with a messy divorce on her own, and her lawyer, who helped immensely, became her best friend in a few months. See, lawyers aren't necessarily as scary as we think they are!

A Lawyer's Point of View

It's not always easy for lawyers either. They deal with cases of heartbreak, families falling apart, immense stress, breakdowns from clients, seeing harsh proof, seeing children go through custody battles, and the cycle goes on day in and day out. Some lawyers double up as counsellors too, when needed. I read an interesting online account of a lawyer who needs help because of how much stress she undergoes in dealing with divorce cases, mostly because she puts on a very brave face in front of her clients, but every couple of months she endures a breakdown as a result of it. Not all lawyers might face the same issue but it's not uncommon. I asked Firoza how she manages to navigate the emotional aspects of it all. She pointed to custody battles as a trigger for her in the initial phase of her career as a divorce lawyer, about six years ago. A case she handled deeply moved her and she found herself breaking down when things got difficult for her client. A lawyer-friend of hers gave her the best advice at that time. 'If you don't isolate and insulate yourself from your work, you can never be objective.' Firoza says it's through practice, time and experience that now she's far more objective, practical and mature. The client walking through the lawyers' offices is in a highly emotional state, and an objective lawyer is a necessity to tackle the situation with a practical approach.

It might help you to remember this, so you can set the correct expectations in your mind about your lawyer as well. They're providing a service to you and that's all it might be. Not letting your expectations stretch beyond that might help you in understanding why a lawyer may not be tending to your emotional needs as well.

Tanya Appachu, popularly known on Instagram as '@yourinstalawyer' walked me through how she does legal consulting. With 180K+ followers and a rapidly growing audience, she makes videos and online content on women's rights, divorce, problems that couples go through, relevant issues in the media today, and so much more. A lot of what she says about divorce is also a result of her parents getting divorced when she was four years old. Tanya is currently not practising in court but takes up consulting with clients before they head to court. 'Let's face it, so many women have no clue where to even begin. So I help them with initial advice and where to go directionally with a divorce. I even connect them to lawyers who can help represent them,' she said. More than society at large, it's sometimes parents who are the first to pose a problem, Tanya concludes after speaking to so many clients wanting to leave marriages. After all, a lot of women who go through abusive marriages just want someone to hear them out. They crave validation, some advice and a lot of empathy. It's also very healing when they actually receive it. 'The funny thing though, is that these are educated people. Commonly heard phrases like, "Go back, it'll be fine. Have a child, it'll be fine" are literally said even today to avoid telling near and dear ones that their daughter is going through a divorce. It's really sad to see this come from educated families, too, who cannot empathize or understand that a marriage cannot work.' Tanya elucidates further on how parents, Indian parents especially, have so much control over us, regardless of how old we are—from food choices, to clothes, to finances and even our partners. She has seen cases where the couple completely stop talking, and the responsibility is passed on to some mama or mami who arranged the wedding, or only the two fathers communicate. She questions the wisdom of this, for so many issues could be solved if the couple sat down to talk instead of giving space to the family to take over. 'I tell my clients that even if two people cannot tolerate each other, just talk about things. Who knows, he/she might also be wanting to opt for a divorce. You won't know that until you talk.'

A common complaint that many clients share with Tanya is that she's far more emotionally available and empathetic than their lawyers. She explains to them that it's not necessary for all lawyers to show emotion or compassion to their clients. Some might, of course. But the main job of the lawyer is to represent their client in court to the best of their ability.

I met Sheila over coffee, a lawyer by profession who'd also gone through a divorce herself. She told me how different it felt when it was her own case versus fighting for others. She had a friend represent her, who did a splendid job of getting it done in just six months' time. Sheila found that it opened up a humane and emotional side of her post the divorce, and she finds it amusing that it changed the way she deals with her cases. It isn't just paperwork for her any more. It's someone's life in her hands.

Janani, an ex-corporate lawyer who quit out of disinterest, went through a fairly simple mutual consent divorce. A renowned lawyer represented her. While speaking about her journey, she raised an important concern. She and her ex-husband went to court for a mutual consent divorce and were still obliged to attend court-mandated counselling. It caused frustration because if two adults are applying for a divorce with consent, then it's likely they've tried everything else before arriving at this decision. During counselling, the couple told the counsellor that they didn't wish to relive talking about their differences and that they were very sure about separating. It wasn't taken too kindly and put them under more stress than required. She was truly intrigued by this loophole, which didn't make sense to her.

Despite the challenge of standing in court, I shall give credit where it is due. It was this time, looking at those in court around me, trying to process my feelings, in the very atmosphere that I was so heartbroken yet amused by, that gave so much clarity about the many things I wanted to do in the future. Standing in a building where at least fifty divorce cases are heard in a day, which has no sense of community, or even a safe space for so many confused folks similar to me, lit a fire inside me to do something truly different. The idea in itself didn't feel radical, but I was sure that there was a massive void and an urgent need for such a concept to exist. It's where I found a new purpose in life. It's where my idea, and grit, for a support group was born.

Counselling: Inside and Outside the Court

One of the more informative calls I had the opportunity to be a part of was with Sadaf Vidha—a therapist, writer and researcher, and also the founder of Guftagu Counselling and Psychotherapy Services, based in Mumbai, Maharashtra. While Sadaf continues her private practice, what really stood out for me was the fact that she also had direct court counselling experience, not as the court-appointed counsellor, but as part of a field action project that appointed her as a third-party counsellor. 'What really lacks in courts is emotional hand-holding,' she says, and that's exactly the gap that her project aimed to fill. Emotional hand-holding would include lending an ear to listen to someone's troubles. Most times, people just want to be heard, rather than getting advice or solutions. Court-appointed counsellors assign cases to the field action project counsellors, thereby helping those entering court get some emotional help as well. However, it is to be noted here that this project was on a temporary basis and will not be found in many courts. It is advisable to find counselling help or therapy outside of the court for the emotional weightlifting one needs during the course of a divorce. Including me, a lot of those who've been in courts have the same concern of reliving the story many times over, which can keep retriggering trauma. However, Sadaf explains that the court counsellors don't necessarily hesitate even if it means the person sitting across from them is reliving trauma over and over again. For them, it's far more important to keep asking the questions to ensure that there's no regret in the future—that every couple walking through the doors of family court is sure of walking out one day with signed divorce papers in their hands.

'The aim is not that of compulsory reconciliation but the focus is on emotional distress reduction,' Sadaf adds, 'and the intent was to bridge as many communication gaps as possible.' Emotional health takes time to build, and this was seen as a good first step to finding a better footing. It's really up to the couple to decide what course of action they want to take. The court counsellor passes on particular cases to other counsellors like Sadaf, who would work out of the family court a few days a week. While this isn't as consistent as a client taking up private therapy sessions, because you'd meet these counsellors only at the court—which would be once in two to three months—it still had a deep impact because empathy at family court is a scarce resource, after all.

While Sadaf was speaking about her private practice, which helps couples as well as individuals in their marriage or divorce, she introduced me to a concept called discernment therapy, which I found interesting to learn about. It's a kind of therapy for couples who know they have problems but don't necessarily want to call it quits. They probably don't know what they want and are in a state of limbo, not being able to move forward. I asked her how couples in situations like this could be helped, and while it's a long process that would change depending on the couple in question, she explained in brief that the role of the therapist is to first figure out if they want to work on the marriage or not. It's only after that exercise that effort comes into the picture. Marriage is indeed hard work, and here's where couples put in that work to either change things around or move on from each other. If there is no consensus on whether they want to be in the marriage or not, then effort might not yield the expected results. Whichever way a couple chooses to go, coping mechanisms become an important pillar of support to lean on.

While I opted for video journaling, gym and other techniques as a coping mechanism, Sadaf had an interesting approach to what these techniques could mean. 'Accept that divorce is a stress-inducing incident,' was the first thing she mentioned. How would we react in any stress-inducing situation? Apply the same to a divorce as well. It's healthy to acknowledge that this is happening and that it might cause a rift in your routine. Accepting that this is okay would be crucial to the process. 'What would you tell your friend going through a divorce? Apply the same to yourself,' she adds. It's very difficult to show compassion to yourself, so treating yourself kindly needs to be regularly practised. It's perfectly all right if productivity goes down, if you lower your expectations of yourself. A divorce puts one through intense stress, so acceptance itself is a form of coping.

When we speak of acceptance, what exactly are we accepting? Sadaf recalls many clients who tend to seek 'revenge', and the resentment and bitterness can have a long-lasting impact on what happens in court as well. The focus on getting back at the other tends to have adverse effects on the one seeking vengeance. Pent-up anger can definitely lead to feelings of wanting to make the one who inflicted pain on you suffer too. A lot of the people I spoke to gave me varying responses as to what constitutes revenge. Some said they will not stop until they feel they've recouped their losses, while others said they felt vengeful but if it doesn't happen, they'll move on. But most of them said that revenge is pretty exhausting and they wouldn't even be able to determine what constitutes 'enough' revenge. Where does one draw the line? Of course, it's subjective to every case and life situation, but more often than not, it invariably takes a toll on the one trying to avenge the other. At the end of the day, how are you prioritizing yourself?

Therapy might help with this and more, to make peace with revenge, anger and unresolved issues that an unhappy marriage could bring to the table. Sadaf believes that medication where needed is extremely beneficial too. Finding a good doctor and believing in their form of healing could be key. It's important to deal with reality in order to heal. 'You have to sit with it, and not just try to jump through hoops.' I found myself rigorously agreeing with her. Since it's not possible to fast-track healing, you need to get into it deeply.

'I have two teenagers and I'm telling them not to get married. Just live in!' says a peppy Nandini Raman, an independent counsellor and therapist. Relationships have become rather flaky and flimsy, so why bother signing a paper and making it more complicated, she ponders. I bonded with her because her sentiments echo my father's views on the institution of marriage, and I was intrigued to see a similar opinion from that generation. As a therapist, Nandini observes a lot of clients come to her needing some hand-holding through their marital problems and looking for ways to help them mend their marriage. If she's approached by an individual, then that person becomes her client. When she's approached by a couple, then the marriage becomes her client, not two individuals. She takes on the role of a moderator and assists them with breaking it down and finding the middle ground.

Nandini narrated a story of how one of her clients was in family court, Chennai, speaking to the counsellor about her case of marital rape being her reason for wanting a divorce. Dismissed, heartbroken and confused by the counsellor's response, who told her it's her duty as the wife to provide sex to her husband, this woman turned to Nandini for consolation and comfort. 'It's a shame that sometimes counsellors at court have no empathy,' Nandini says, while also speaking about the importance of taking care of one's mental health while dealing with highly volatile situations before and during a divorce.

A marriage needn't fall apart only because of divorce. So many smaller issues could cause a gap in understanding and communication. Nandini finds that most of her clients struggle with how they'd make their parents understand. Often, parents would take themselves as examples, describing how they got through problems no matter what. 'Romance might not have been a big part of that generation's priorities but it is the case today,' she continues. A lot of couples find that their physical needs are as important as their emotional ones. On more than one occasion, it's been noted that the previous generation fails to comprehend what an important role intimacy plays.

A number of women I spoke to repeatedly mentioned the role of therapy in the process of healing, and I can't help wondering why something so magical and powerful has been so stigmatized. Mental health is just as important as physical health. However, this might require a whole other book.

I started therapy long after my divorce ended. At the end of 2019, when I felt a lot more grounded and ready to face my demons, I had my first session. Just like I spent time finding a lawyer, I also took time to find a therapist I could trust. I took online video sessions, which were so much easier for me to do. I had very specific reasons for reaching out to a therapist, and I was able to articulate exactly where I needed help as well. It took months of work but therapy definitely helped me untangle some of the knots of confusion in my head, many of which I didn't even realize existed. Trauma is sometimes stored in knots in our bodies as well, and not just in our mind. I learnt a lot of simple techniques for breathing, concentrating, processing and so much more from a rather lovely therapist. Therapists have a way of gently digging into invisible wounds and then also teaching us how to work through the pain that follows. But once the pain subsides, you feel so much better and lighter. I'll forever be thankful to myself for making this investment and following through. I'd highly recommend it to everybody—divorce or not.

But especially for divorce. Because no divorce is easy.

Coping with Divorce

28 November 2018 seemed to take forever to come. The months leading up to it were the hardest I'd faced in my life so far. I hope I don't have to go through anything as severe again. I suffered from psychosomatic pain, which meant I woke up on many days with inexplicable pain that would stun me. I'd sit for hours in one place and stare at the wall. I'd cry. I'd cry a lot. There was no reason to stop crying.

Like any other human, I would watch Netflix for entertainment. One show, *Grace & Frankie*, had a huge impact on me during this tough time. In one scene, Frankie speaks about video journaling as a way to cope, and she takes her phone out and starts talking to the camera. I recalled this scene while sitting alone and bawling my eyes out one afternoon. I couldn't control the crying so I decided to give her idea a try. I turned on my phone, placed it against a water bottle and started talking. I blabbered, I cried, I laughed, I swore and I said unbelievably evil things I'd never otherwise say out loud. I made really stupid jokes, and so much more for about an hour. It didn't make any sense but it helped me so much. I had stopped crying, and I definitely felt better. I continued to do this whenever I needed to. The video journal created a safe, non-judgemental space for myself, consisting of only me. I didn't realize how much it was needed until I had done it. Healing isn't linear, of course, and this contributed greatly to getting me where I wanted to be.

My closest friends told me they couldn't recognize who I had become, and they were worried that I'd deteriorated so rapidly. I had no answers or solutions. All I could come up with was that this was temporary and I'd be fine again. I wasn't entirely sure if that was the truth, but saying it was a way to reassure myself as well. In between two court dates, my friends whisked me off for a beach vacation. I couldn't have been more grateful for that break. I distinctly remember one evening that stood out for me that week. I swam in the ocean, floating in the blue waters, watching the marine life beneath and the sunset above on the horizon. It was the calmest I'd felt in four years. I let loose, shut my thoughts off, and just wanted to experience those moments to the maximum that I could. During my three hours in the water, I watched the sun go to bed and stepped out only when the waves became more risky. Something changed that day. I released some anger, hurt and grief into the ocean and felt lighter afterwards. This feeling remains with me to this day.

When I talked to my lawyer for the first time, I was initially able to collect myself and stay calm. As the months rolled by, my strength and willpower started to deteriorate. I became exhausted, sad and hurt. I wasn't able to accept the fact that the whole concept of falling in love and the ability to build a life with someone was reduced to nothing but dry, emotionless sheets of paper. My mind was almost constantly spinning in a state of high anxiety.

The more words I filled into the petition draft, the more I had to relive the past. It made me feel detached from the present. But when I saw it in writing with each emotion explicitly stated for anyone to read, it also hit me very differently. I realized I'd started losing myself, and felt unrecognizable. My interests dwindled, and I didn't feel like putting effort into any form of self-care either. I couldn't remember who I was and I didn't like who I was becoming. Everything that was happening was just too overwhelming. I needed an outlet, something that would help me channel these feelings. I also knew that if I let things fester instead of resolving them, my decision would come back later to bite me.

A close relative recommended meditation. Even the thought of meditating put me off. Around the same time, a friend told me to hit the gym. I shunned it for a while, thinking it was too much effort. But one rainy day, I went to the gym out of sheer boredom. And there was no looking back. Running on the treadmill gave me more peace than anything else. I'd blast music into my eardrums, turn up the treadmill, and run like a bear was chasing me through a forest. This became a habit and one that truly helped me. We all have coping mechanisms that work uniquely for us and this was mine. Each time I'd return from court or my lawyer's office, I'd run extra that day. Another unexpected advantage of this was that my sleep started improving. Gym fatigue meant I had fewer nightmares, and thus, fewer late nights. Feeling physically fit was the last reason for going to the gym; changing my mental health was the first. And it really worked!

In between work and gym, I had to continue preparing for court. Nothing was really private any more. Everything was a transaction that was recorded on paper for I-don't-know-how-many people to read. Exercise helped considerably, but on many days, nothing could stop the storm in my head. I couldn't fight it. I just had to let it wash over me. I wanted to keep sleeping and not wake up. I didn't want to face this. I just wanted it to be over.

I just wanted it to be over.

Just be over.

Over.

Almost at the Finish Line

Somewhere in the middle of the proceedings, I felt exceptionally overwhelmed. We were discussing the way forward, and the lawyer and her legal team had multiple suggestions that seemed complicated and would mean more time spent in court. Just the thought of that gave me anxiety attacks. I took many days to think about what the next steps should be, and the pressure to plan the path ahead was mounting. I didn't feel ready. I called my friend, crying that I was not able to understand how to decide the right course of action. I was literally standing at a fork in the road. She calmed me down, got me to stop crying and then offered to put me in touch with her uncle, a retired judge who had spent most of his life witnessing couples end their marriages. I took her up on the offer, and that one phone call turned my life around for the better. He spoke to me patiently, equating my needs to those of his niece. What followed in that phone call was basically an outcome of his years of experience and the empathy in his heart. He didn't tell me what to do or what not to do. Instead, he asked me questions that I answered promptly, letting me draw my own conclusions. He did it with such ease. The relief that I felt is something I cannot put into words. I broke down during the phone call, thanking him for offering me this clarity. He didn't stop at that. He also motivated me enough to believe that soon this would all be over, and I'd be able to live the best life ahead. It's been almost four years since that call, and I can still remember his calm voice and his wise words ringing in my ears. I identify as an atheist but from that evening onwards, he was my God.

I sat across from the counsellor at court one evening, a couple of months after that phone call, waiting all day for my turn. I felt extremely impatient by this time and wanted to finalize the proceedings. I didn't want to discuss the past all over again, and I definitely didn't want to keep revisiting the court. I requested a speedy end to this process, so we could all happily head home. Calling it a request is probably putting it too lightly. I begged. I was glad to see the counsellor show me his human side and offer to help me out. It's not really possible to speed things up in court since there are many due processes that need to be followed. But what could speed it up is more intense counselling sessions that didn't just focus on the past but a discussion about the future so things could come to a close.

It would be another three months before my divorce would actually conclude. Time went by in a blur. Every day when I woke up, I wanted to be done and be free. I hadn't been this impatient for anything else in my life. But it was a phenomenal feeling to see light at the end of the tunnel. From wondering if that year would ruin me forever to actually finding hope in small pockets, I was caught by surprise and I loved it. Very slowly, I was starting to regain some confidence in myself. I started smiling every once in a while. I could even sleep better.

January went by and I was granted the divorce on 23 January 2019. Oh, what a day! For about ten days before this, every time I imagined holding that final document, I'd burst into tears of happiness. Maybe I overdid the drama in my head but when I actually stood in court and was told I was done, I was beaming with joy. I couldn't wipe the smile off my face. I didn't feel anything other than relief. It felt like a sort of body pain where a weight was being lifted off. I was light-headed and dizzy. When I walked out of the judge's chambers, I locked eyes with my parents, who were sitting patiently outside in the waiting area. I threw my arms up in the air and gave them a thumbs up, a smile still plastered across my face. They returned it with claps I couldn't hear but could feel.

'IT'S OVER! IT'S FINALLY OVER!'

I copy pasted this message to over fifteen of my close friends, who were waiting in different parts of the world to hear from me. There were celebrations all round. They'd seen me go through so much. They knew 'congratulations!' was the only response I was looking for. I sat in a cafe with my parents and my lawyer and had a cup of overpriced coffee as a treat. It had been an hour since we'd left the court and I was still smiling. Even my parents were relieved. It was a long journey back home, and I was exhausting my phone battery texting each of my friends, endlessly bombarding them with everything that I was feeling.

It was really important for me to set boundaries here as well, particularly with family. I didn't want curiosity seeping in. I wanted full control over who knew my story and who didn't. There was no need to tell everybody everything. I sent messages to family groups about the finality of the divorce and let them know that I was happy and safe at home, with my parents. I also added in bold to not ask what happened and why I chose a divorce. I didn't want to get into that. I added one more line: 'Please say congratulations, don't say you're sorry.' I guess the trick worked. I got many replies congratulating me. How many of those were genuine and how many were because I'd asked for it, I really don't know. Honestly, I couldn't care less. To my parents' friends and well-wishers, we said the same via email. The boundaries were kept intact, the medium of communication varied.

While my parents were extremely supportive of my decision, I need to mention my maternal grandmother who was particularly loving and kind to me through this. When she first saw me at my parents' home after the separation, she burst into tears. Her concern was for me, not the label of a divorce or how society would perceive it. Later that night, she sent us a text on a WhatsApp group, which must have taken her at least twenty-five minutes to type out—'GRBR, good riddance to bad rubbish. Love you.' I felt like I was on top of the world! If my eighty-two-year-old grandmother could understand what this meant to me, I knew I would be able to carry on with life on my terms.

Celebrations: A Divorce Party

To counter the restlessness with something exciting, I started planning a divorce party for myself. This was when things started looking up for me. In my head, there was no doubt that this would be a celebration for me. After almost three years of shouldering stress that almost changed me completely, I finally had the chance to redeem myself and prove to the world that I'm not going to buckle under the pressure. The divorce party was not just a celebration of my new life, but also a tribute to my friends, who stood by me through thick and thin, boosting me up, holding me as I wept and cheering me on for every small win. They deserved it. I'm not great with Excel sheets even today, but I did open one to start planning the party. The end was in sight, which meant I could put a tentative date to the event. Friends needed time to travel to Mumbai as well. 10 February 2019. It was decided.

I bought myself the prettiest yellow cape dress as a gift. Yellow is such a bright, shiny, happy colour, and that's how I wanted to waltz into my grand new life. The little gift bags for my friends included a hand-painted cup, a plant, a handwritten letter and a personalized T-shirt that read 'Shaadu is free!'. The party would be held in my office space, so I slowly started thinking about the decor as well: a banner, with a few cheeky phrases, was prepared on funky artwork—all done from scratch—and there was a piece of plain chart paper, for all my friends to kiss and leave their lip imprint, because why the hell not? Planning this event infused life into me again, and gave me something to look forward to. I wasn't thinking of my future beyond 10 February. All I wanted was to get there. To see my friends all together, to get the warmest hugs, to sit around and talk.

10 February was fast approaching, and to say I was excited is a big understatement. Gym had become a healthy habit I didn't want to let go of, and I continued to work out as I did before, but without the stress of a court date or a call from my lawyer. That feeling of freedom is something I hope I never forget or take for granted. I was exhilarated, beyond joyful, and knew that this hadn't come easily to me, so here I was ready to savour every single second.

I booked a parlour appointment on the 10th for a haircut and blow-dry. It doesn't take a million bucks to feel like a million bucks. I strutted out of the salon and back to the party venue, flipping my hair around dramatically. I'd spent all of my time after work hours for the past few days decking out the living room of my office, the stage for the much-awaited party. It looked stunning.

There were fifteen people on the invite list; thirteen were going to show up. All my women. Some already knew each other, while some only knew of each other. Female friendships and the solidarity of sisterhood truly got me through this. We were ready to celebrate together in pomp and splendour. I knew that my friends had also been through a lot of stress with me. It was a celebration, no doubt, but it was also the closure we all needed. The decree only comes a close second.

My yellow gang showed up! That night with my girlfriends stands out as one of the best moments in my thirty years of existence so far. Dancing is a beautiful form of expression, and like many other non-dancers, I put my two left feet to good use, unconcerned about how I looked. We had a fantastic cake, vegan pizzas and popcorn to fortify us. After midnight, when the dancers were worn out, we sat in the dim light and spoke about what this closure meant to us. It was so heart-warming, surreal and beautiful. I took the longest time to finish my speech, thanking each one for her contribution, for they are the water that floats my boat.

I woke up the next morning and bid goodbye to my friends as they left. It was sad to see them go, of course. But it also left me filled with so much positivity and zeal to begin my new life. At work that day, I wanted to do something that signified closure just for myself. I remembered a gift that was lying around—a book of seed papers. I took a pen and wrote out every single negative thought I'd had in the last few years, tore up the pieces and planted them in the ground nearby. This was a symbolic reminder that there are silver linings to every dark cloud. The seed paper might have had unpleasant words written on it but it would ultimately flower into something beautiful and useful. This was the closure I wanted and this was the closure I deserved.

What a peaceful, beautiful new beginning.

I hope this encourages you to celebrate yourself too. This party gave me the conviction and confidence that I was going to be all right. If you've gone through a divorce, it's likely you've been in a very stressful situation. Start your new life with a clean slate. Don't let anybody make you feel like you don't deserve it. Give yourself a pat on the back for getting through it, and treat your friends and those who truly stood by you to something special. One night dedicated to honouring yourself can only do you (and them) good. It also gives you the opportunity to look back at this celebration as a fond memory every year, and I promise you, you'll be delighted to discover just how far you've come!

And you know, new beginnings always deserve cake.

After receiving my divorce decree, I was on cloud nine. I was beaming with happiness for months. I was focusing on myself. I did everything in my power to change my life and curate it so that it was exactly how I liked it. I just wanted to be free, and fearless. As an entrepreneur, I worked hard on my business. I reconnected with friends with new vigour. I spent time with family, worked out at the gym, sang more and opened myself up to new possibilities and experiences. I felt unstoppable. I knew this euphoria would be short-lived, but I wasn't going to let that put a dampener on anything I wanted to do. I was experiencing a once-in-a-lifetime sort of joy, so I wanted to cherish every moment.

Life after Divorce

They say if one door closes, another opens. That's what happened to me. From January 2019, my life changed for the better. When I was sitting in court and watching the people around me, my mind was filled to the brim with thoughts. They were so overwhelming that I almost forgot why I was there. I would often look at my parents and wonder how much more of a mess I'd have been had they not been at court. I will never forget the sacrifices they made to ensure I was never alone in court or elsewhere. I am so grateful to be born to them. My mother took on the role of a best friend who cared for me, cooked comforting meals, went on walks and watched TV shows with me as a form of distraction, while my father, on the other hand, helped me with every aspect of the legalities, ensured I was comfortable at home and always asked me to believe that a much better life awaited me. It was such a privilege that they were there. Looking around me in court, there were several others without that kind of support. I tried speaking to a few people there, but in my highly emotional state, I wasn't able to fully empathize without feeling a sense of crippling anxiety. One scene I will never forget is giving a tissue I had in my bag to a woman crying profusely in the washroom. I didn't know what to say to her. I didn't want to ask. She didn't talk either but our eyes met. I handed her the tissue with a wry smile. I truly hope she's doing better today. In case you're reading this or even relate to being that woman in court, then I'm sending you a big hug.

My conversation with Sarita in that cafe had changed my mindset while I went through the proceedings. It opened up a plethora of possibilities for me. I knew I wanted to set up a space for people to come and share their experiences. Divorces can be deeply isolating. The power of familiarity could make a world of difference for someone needing it. Although I knew what I wanted to do, I didn't know where to begin.

I vowed that one day, I'd be a Sarita for someone else. On the day of my divorce, I wanted to speak about it online—to test the waters and see what the response would be on Instagram. I was sceptical, but hey, curiosity got the better of me. The thought of my engagement ring had been lingering in my mind for a while. After my separation and before the divorce, I was still wearing the ring. It was a daily reminder of my earlier life. I wanted to take it off. One fine day, I finally did. I thought it would make me feel empowered and free, but instead I felt empty and lonely, and my finger itched for the ring. On a trip to my home town, Chennai, I found a ring in a shop there which was a perfect fit for the same empty finger. I shared a photo of my hand, with freshly painted nails and that ring and wrote: 'I learnt that I'm my best companion and I will be able to fill in the empty blanks in life on my own. With little dependency on another human. I wore this ring and felt oddly complete, and liberated. I felt independent. And it sealed the deal. I got some form of closure.' I was overwhelmingly surprised when the post received 700+ likes and over 200 comments from friends, well-wishers and complete strangers telling me I'm strong, celebrating my new life, congratulating me, calling me an independent woman, and sending me so much love. I couldn't believe the positivity it attracted. The numbers are not important compared to the quality of support it received organically.

A day later, my inbox was flooded with stories from acquaintances and strangers alike, telling me how the story of the ring resonated with them because of their experiences. I didn't probe into any story. The number of people opening up and sharing stories, through the limited reach I had online, was overwhelming. If this was what I could rake up as an individual, then the number of real stories spanning the country would be mind-boggling. My head was spinning in various directions and I took a step back to understand what I really wanted to do here.

For a few days after my successful divorce party, several pictures continued to make the rounds on the 'gram, and once again, they were extremely well received. Nobody expected a life event like a divorce to be something that was shared, let alone celebrated. This again was met with rapturous applause and cheers. I went all out in sharing pictures, videos and little stories from that night. My friends completely supported me, and the reaction to this party was exactly the validation I needed that I was heading in the right direction. I knew I wanted to do a lot for this cause. I didn't know exactly what that would be but something was brewing.

Could I try to look for positive implications? I knew I could and wanted to draw it out of myself, no matter how hard it felt. But the truth is, when I tried, it was much easier than I expected it to be. The process was also healing. What I did know was that I wanted to focus on healing, the path to navigate stigma, and how we can collectively change divorce into something that's merely a life choice and not just a negative experience. I wanted to speak openly about a taboo topic through the lens of Indian society.

The Birth of 'Divorce Is Normal'

While thinking of a caption for one of the posts I was writing, I noted down that divorce needs to be a completely normal thing, not something to be afraid of. And those who get divorced aren't 'abnormal'. I didn't think of it as a campaign or anything larger than life back then. I just thought it'd be a good hashtag to document my thoughts in one place. Hence, #DivorceIsNormal came to be. The more it took shape, the more I wanted this to be something anybody could use, not just me. The whole point of speaking about a stigmatized subject was to open up minds and hope that the hushed-up topic could be exposed. What probably began by an individual, but eventually branched out to a community. I opened up a page in the notes app on my phone and wrote down topics I wanted to share and talk more about. I surprised myself with how much I already knew and how many opinions I'd formed without actively knowing I had. But here I was, exhilarated and fully pumped up to build a new voice for anybody going through a divorce or who had previously undergone one. I had a singular goal—to never feel sidelined again.

Soon after the excitement about the divorce party started to die down, I got back into the zone of writing about serious topics. The more I wrote, the more I thought; the more I could opine, the more I could grow. A couple of posts later, a brand expressed interest in featuring me for a campaign that spoke about 'flawed' women taking control of their narrative. It was quite an elaborate shoot, and the noob in me was highly excited by what was happening. I sat in front of a camera in a pretty little cafe and spoke about the divorce. It was the first time I was speaking in front of a camera, except for the video journaling, and to strangers who were standing behind the camera and listening to me speak. I felt so self-conscious about using the word divorce, but it also came with a deep sense of surety and confidence I hadn't felt before. I left the set that day beaming with pride. I did it! I wanted to find pockets of happiness and I was indeed finding them. The goal of starting to talk about this online was only partly for myself. The larger aspiration was to get others talking about it too. Unless we collectively speak about a taboo, things will remain static. What joy I found in trying to navigate this!

The stories pouring into my inbox only multiplied by the day. A girl told me that it felt like a 'release into the world' when she shared her story with me, even if the DM had only been between us. If you think about it, a lot of us feel the urge to write to someone we can relate to when their words strike a chord in us. I received a flurry of messages with different emotions—from those looking for lawyers, to those who wanted to know about life after a divorce. Others wanted to know what happened had to me, or they just wanted to be heard or to share, while many were just kind and appreciative of me addressing this topic.

To keep my sanity intact, I took breaks from Instagram and continued helping those texting me as much as my bandwidth allowed. I had my fair share of people asking me what had happened and why I'd decided to end my marriage. I had a very simple answer and I kept repeating it for months together. Do not ask me what happened. If I wanted to share it publicly, I would have. I choose not to—not through social media, not even through this book. If I continue to keep harping on about the past, how will I move on to other things in the future? I wanted to speak about divorce openly only because I wanted to shatter the stigma, crack open conversations that might be uncomfortable but necessary, and make it as normal as a marriage is. My aim was to take voices like yours and mine and make us feel heard in society. The intent was not to emphasize what happened to me but to normalize what's happening to thousands across the country. If marriage is accepted so widely, then divorce needs to be as well.

I continued ranting about my thoughts for a couple of months, engaging with the community I was trying to build, empathizing with others and keeping the conversation alive. I'd taken a few calls from some friends as well who I met via social media. I sat up a few nights helping people through panic attacks and bawling sessions, and offering general support. I stretched myself thin but couldn't stop since I was getting emotionally involved with every story. Then came a day when I woke up one morning, opened Instagram and saw about eight pictures sent to my inbox. It was a woman sharing pictures of her terribly bruised body parts. She'd been beaten black and blue the previous night, and she had sent me these images along with a message, 'I have no support, what do I do? I want to die.'

My morning came to a halt, and I was suddenly wide awake. It was one of the first things I was seeing that morning and I was shaken. I didn't know her identity or the city she lived in. This woman was in pain and desperate, and I did not know how I could help. I spent that day in emotional turmoil, thinking of her, and many other women in abusive households without the means to leave for safer spaces. This, coupled with so many other stories I'd listened to and absorbed, brought me to my knees. That day, I was triggered beyond my control and I broke down. I was left with a deep sense of helplessness and anger at how prevalent abuse is in so many households. I was horrified to realize that divorce bears the weight of stigma but abuse roams free. The excruciating depth of the problem hit me very hard. I found it hard to fathom the length and breadth of how far this travels. How it hits so many homes, so many families.

This was the rude awakening I needed to take a break and distance myself from the trauma around me. Unless I could take care of myself, I couldn't find the energy to continue talking about divorce openly, or helping those who truly needed it. It was benefiting many others, and I wanted to keep that channel open, particularly for women, who found it easy to open up to someone who had been through something similar and wouldn't judge. I didn't want a single person reaching out to feel like they didn't have the support they needed. The legal process is heart-wrenching as it is. The least I could do was lend a helpful ear. The mistake I made, however, is that I didn't know my boundaries then. After seeing the abused woman's photos, I took a few days off social media to take stock of my mental health and reassess what I was doing. I wanted to shake off the feeling of helplessness and convert it into something tangible that I could offer. I needed to rethink my new boundaries. If you're considering offering help to someone else in need, remember that taking care of yourself is of the utmost importance. Give yourself that space and time to heal so you are able to help another person with a layer of detachment in your head. This way, you'll be far more useful.

A lot of social proof existed that #DivorceIsNormal was growing in size and numbers. It gave me immense joy every time I saw the hashtag being populated by more posts that were not mine. Initially, I saw a friend or two writing, and then it expanded. Discovering new accounts who were pouring their hearts out—writing about stigma, talking about what happened to them, single parents sharing their accounts and women writing about dating as a divorced individual—continued to be such a wonderful feeling. The movement was growing, and the hashtag didn't just belong to me. Community is everything.

The first thing I had to work on was the guilt I felt about putting myself first. 2019 was a year of redemption and a new life for me. I didn't want to waste it by doing the right things the wrong way. A fresh start needed fresh thoughts as well. I opened up on Instagram stories about this as well, talking about how I'd been relentlessly working on things for a few months and the toll it took on me. Given the amazing community I was building, I only found love and acceptance for my thoughts. It was what I needed to hear for the guilt to slowly fade away. It was a validation that had meaning attached to it.

This, in no way, stopped me from continuing to share my thoughts via posts. I learnt that I have the capacity to listen to people without getting entwined in their story. It took some practice but I was eventually able to crack the formula. I needed to harden myself, for every single day I had messages from someone new who wanted support of some kind. I also felt a sense of responsibility to do better because while I was living a new life, others weren't. I couldn't let my emotions get in the way of support for someone else. After all, they reached out for their own peace. It's their story, not mine.

Generally, many things get better with time, and this did too. I'm so glad, since it meant I didn't have to stop myself from discovering more ways in which I could support women. One day, I wanted to have a support group of my own.

And I worked really hard towards what I wanted.

Setting Up a Divorce Support Group

By September 2019, six months of finding my freedom and voice, the copious excitement levels had begun to reduce. My feet were back on firm ground. I had a better grip on reality. I understood what I wanted to do and felt confident that I was doing something right. I was ready to take the plunge into moving the conversations and connections offline. Even though it is great that the world is so well connected digitally, making life easier in multiple ways, there is something special about meeting in person. I floated the idea to a few of my friends and started small groups with people I already knew, just to get a sense of whether I was really prepared to sit through a session without letting my emotions get the better of me.

Asking for help isn't a piece of cake. There's a common misconception that it is a sign of weakness. There's also a lot of shame associated with it. To accept help is acknowledging that you don't have control over a certain aspect of your life, which is possibly the main reason why therapy is still not widely accepted. 'What's the big deal? I can take care of myself' is a very common notion that so many hold. I'm not invalidating anybody's feelings. I'm saying that sometimes we don't even realize we need help because we haven't received the conditioning that help is beneficial. Most of us were conditioned to believe that seeking help indicates weakness. And how many of us voluntarily want to look weak?

I turned twenty-eight that October and promised myself that going forward, I'll do as much as possible for this cause, relentlessly. But the bigger promise to myself was that I will take care of myself through this process. I really dislike going back on my word, so I absolutely had to honour this promise.

It took a few weeks to scout for the ideal venue to host the first support group meeting—cosy, small, welcoming, warm and comfortable. Where could I even begin looking for this space? Most studios charged by the hour, and I didn't intend to charge those coming to share their experiences. While I was searching, I ended up speaking to an acquaintance who owned a sweet little restaurant right in the heart of the city. He offered his space for free, on Sundays, before the restaurant opened. We wouldn't have access to food, but we'd get water and comfortable seating. That was more than generous enough!

Now that the venue was set, I needed a list of participants. Nervous and jittery, I made a post and shared it on Instagram. I wanted to cap the event at fifteen people, since anything more than that becomes too much of a crowd, which could mean that not everybody gets the chance to talk and share their thoughts. 24 November 2019 was an incredibly special day in my life.

I could barely sleep the previous night. I was excited, and nervous energy had curled up in a ball inside my stomach. I could use the venue from 9 a.m., for about two hours. We had to clear the space before they opened for the day. Once I reached the venue, I stood outside and took a deep breath before entering. I had sixteen confirmed slots and I had to put on hold many others who wanted to be there. That morning, four of them cancelled. I decided to focus on the twelve who actually made it. The participants at that day's event were all women, though the registrations were open to all genders. We rearranged the furniture to make a cosy little circle such that we could all see and hear each other. Once the women started walking in and I started greeting them and introducing myself, there was no room for any nervousness—just the feeling of wanting to fully experience our time together for the next two hours with no inhibitions, judgements or negativity. After the initial introductions, we found a spot to comfortably sit in. I'd requested everyone to put their phones away and just let loose and breathe comfortably. I was surprised at how beautifully it flowed. I gave the twelve beautiful ladies a small introduction about why I was doing this and how I got started, along with anecdotes from my own life that brought me to that very moment.

Among these twelve women, there was a twenty-two-year-old, as well as a sixty-year-old and everybody else in between. Your age doesn't matter. We all deserve a chance to feel heard and supported. I requested those who wanted to talk to feel free to share but not to feel obligated to do or say anything just because they had come to the meeting. We heard twelve stories brimming with strength and grit. Not all of them were divorced either; a couple of them were in the middle of their court proceedings. A turning point during this meeting was when one woman broke down while describing what a tough time she was facing at court. Suddenly, we weren't strangers who'd just met an hour ago. Nobody knew the other until that morning. But when this person started crying, we all took turns to reassure her. We were once in her place too, so we knew what to say and what not to say. If others around her could move on to better health, a better mental space and more, she could too. We took turns to hug her and give her the best support possible. The energy in the room left me with goosebumps. The familiarity that I knew was so powerful was actually manifesting in front of my eyes. I couldn't believe it. When I wasn't speaking, I took the time to absorb all the energy around me. Feminine strength filled me with a kind of hope that I've never felt before.

While we reassured her, it segued wonderfully into each of us sharing our coping mechanisms when we go through something extremely tough. Someone took medication, another created art. One chose to travel, another to play music, and we heard about such varied experiences. Each of us had a smile on our faces, and I could tell that every single one in the group felt the atmosphere of support I had sought to create. The oldest among us, the sixty-year-old, told us that she had been unsure about coming to meet a group of strangers to speak about her private life. But her daughter had seen my previous posts and had assured her that this was a safe space, and who knew, she might just like it. Did she like it? She loved it, and she said it out loud. We discussed difficult situations, trauma, guilt and more, but it ended with hope and positivity. It was electrifying.

Two hours slipped into three, and our hosts were kind enough to let us continue. We walked into the room as strangers that day, but we walked out feeling so connected. I call myself a writer, but I can't put into words what it felt like when I hugged every single one of them and thanked them for making the morning so memorable and empowering. That's the power of community. Put yourself in a room full of people who believe you, who support you and understand what you've gone through. That's the validation and support that will uplift you and make you feel whole. We were left with the conviction that the power of familiarity could give the boost of confidence to propel us forward.

I was full of enthusiasm after the first support group meeting. I mentally walked back in time to my life just a year before that, which was so messy and affected by court proceedings and the related anxiety they induced. And here I was, a year later, sharing my healing with others and providing a space that was much needed. Healing isn't linear, and on this day, I felt I had taken a giant leap forward for myself.

I recounted that morning to many of my friends and my parents, and I couldn't stop talking about it. Support groups aren't common in the country and the concept itself was something I'd only encountered in movies. But here I was, running one of my own. When I was in court in 2018, I wanted to find such a group to help me move forward. I'd spoken to some people individually which had helped a lot, but just imagining that at a group level felt cathartic to me in many ways. Although I researched this thoroughly, I couldn't find anything. I joined a Facebook group for divorced women, run by an NGO in New York, and while it was wonderful to see so many women open up and talk about their lives, I felt that the context of Indian social stigma was missing, along with discussions on how to navigate it. I continued to participate in that group as much as I could, only becoming more convinced that a support group in *this* country for divorced people was not a luxury, but a necessity.

I wanted to expand the group as much as I could, so I started conducting more sessions and my confidence grew. After locking in an idea of the format, the disclaimers and rules that needed to be announced, how to divide time without sounding insensitive and also to give a general direction on what we were gathered there for, I was ready to take it a notch up. I also conducted a few smaller groups of people in cafes, open areas and rooftops. Because this was something I spoke of online, it became easier to find venues to host the events. I began connecting with people to ask for help when I needed it, and I am very grateful for the support I received from so many different people spanning across cities. Despite a few hiccups, I managed to connect with smaller groups in every city I travelled to in that short period. I even met some individually, to hear them out. I'd share what worked for me and what didn't, offer them the best services for lawyers and therapists, or just sit with them and listen to their story.

The Power of Support Systems

I speak highly of support systems. I'm a huge believer in them. But I often hear this, which I'd love to address here as well: 'My friend is in an abusive marriage, and I keep asking her to leave him, but she just wouldn't listen!'

Now, you cannot force someone to apply for a divorce when you're not one half of the marriage. If you're a friend looking to help a loved one, it's important for you to know that you cannot force things. It's easy to spot abuse when you're a third person viewing a relationship as a spectator. It's completely different when you're in the marriage, trying to comprehend so many things at the same time. I took two years to walk out of my marriage and nobody could have made it happen faster. I needed the time, space and strength to come to terms with the situation. Similarly, we each have a different timeline we operate on, and just because you, as a friend or a family member, can see things clearly, it does not mean the person facing abuse owes it to you to leave.

I've listened to frustrated friends and family members who, out of deep concern, tend to be irritable because they can't understand why this person they know and love is choosing to suffer and just can't seem to get out of the marriage. Don't get me wrong. I'm not saying you cannot give advice. Please lend a helping hand, a few thoughtful words and many hugs. But you cannot direct the separation or the divorce. It's also not your place to feel frustrated or angry because someone you know won't just pack their bags and leave. It takes a lot of introspection, time, effort and planning.

What you can do is gently present them with options and help them take one step at a time. If you tell a scared, manipulated, abused person to file for a divorce, you're likely to scare them off. Start small. Ask them to stay at a different location for a few days or gift them a couple of therapy sessions to get started. Step by step, you will gain their trust, and they will realize that it's a slow process to reach the destination of divorce, rather than one giant quick leap which feels too daunting to take. Hold their hand, offer comfort and let them take their time. Patience is what will see you and your loved one through a tricky situation like this.

At the end of 2019, I got the most incredible opportunity to speak at a renowned public forum. TEDx had invited me to present the work I was doing and why I thought it was relevant. Me? Give a TEDx talk? When I saw the message, I thought my friends were pranking me. But they weren't, and it was something I had to seriously prepare for. I was really excited. I'd like to once again thank

Flame University, Pune for that incredible evening of 6 December. I'd written a speech, edited it so many times, made little notes on chits of paper, got a T-shirt with 'divorce is normal' written on it, borrowed a friend's black blazer, polished a pair of wedges and set off to conquer the stage. I was extremely aware of the importance of this speech, which was a golden chance to spread that feeling of community I was working towards and to tell society that divorce is isolating, so please be kinder to others. It set the stage to put divorce in the limelight and take a big step towards shattering the heavy stigma surrounding it. Divorce was getting a leg-up. The butterflies in my tummy vanished the minute I stood on stage and started talking. All that preparation made it easy. I shared with the audience, and on video, the reasons I thought it was important to speak about divorce. I took the opportunity to share anecdotes that many other divorced people might find comforting and relatable, the importance of setting up a support group in this country, shattering the stigma of divorce, and the realization of how ingrained it is in this country to treat divorce as a taboo. What was beautiful was that after the speech, when I sat down for dinner with a few students who were eager to ask me a bunch of questions, two of them took me aside. One asked me how to help her aunt and uncle cope in a terrible marriage and what she should do, and more importantly, what she shouldn't. The other asked me what she needed to find out about her boyfriend before getting married so she could be sure of making the right choice.

The interactions after this talk made one thing glaringly obvious to me—that divorce is a topic that's relevant in almost every public space. You could walk into any room with people of different ages and speak about divorce, and there's always someone who relates to it, or someone known to them who comes to their mind when this topic is brought up. It's so prevalent, yet so stigmatized. As I mentioned earlier, where marriage is prevalent, divorce should be spoken about too.

TEDx was further proof that there's a lot of potential to branch out in the work I was doing, and it reinforced my aim to reach out to many more people who require this support and help.

Going forward, I truly hope to see many more people open up in public spaces about how deeply the divorce stigma is entrenched in our society, and how standing together against it can be the most empowering way to eradicate it.

Divorce during Covid

When the COVID-19 pandemic shook the world, the sudden lockdown resulted in the courts being shut, which caused tremendous disruption in many households, marriages and individuals' lives. Those already in the process of a divorce faced unprecedented delays. Those who were planning a divorce had to stay put because the courts were shut. The ones who probably suffered the most were those stuck at home in abusive marriages. For a lot of such women, office hours were the only hours they got to themselves. With working from home becoming the new normal, it became increasingly difficult for them to function. They couldn't even go out for a walk to let off steam.

I moved the support group online. Like everything else that went digital, so did support for divorce. I divided participants into groups of fifteen for each weekend and arranged sessions on Google Meet. I followed the same template as the in-person meetings, except this was on a screen. One advantage was that there was no restriction regarding the location. The group welcomed people from around the world, for divorce is pretty much universal.

An incident that really broke our hearts during one of the weekend sessions was one of those life moments that felt like a mental earthquake. After a few other participants spoke, this girl unmuted herself and asked if she could speak. She did speak but she was whispering. She apologized for how soft she sounded and then said while sobbing, 'My husband is in a meeting outside and he cannot know I'm in this group. I'm hiding under the bed and speaking to you. I cannot switch on my video either because I have some fresh bruises from last night.' She eventually did switch on her video and showed us her plight. A few of us were moved to tears as we tried to absorb the shock of it together. We might know this to be a generalized reality, but when you see it unfold in front of your eyes and hear someone's experience of it in real time, it sends a shiver down your spine. This was in the middle of a very strict lockdown. Where could she even go?

I think it'd be safe to say that was one of the biggest issues during the pandemic and lockdown—so many silent sufferers across the country, and even the world, who didn't have a way out. We saw a rise in more such groups coming together online, for the least we could do for humanity was to stick together and be there for each other during the toughest of times.

Every Sunday between 3 and 7 p.m., a group of people huddled together in a safe space to pour their hearts out and share their stories of equal parts misery and joy. We heard stories of heartbreak, of hope, of neglected children, of supportive parents, of unsupportive parents, of education, of frustration, of lack of finances, of complicated questions to which answers didn't seem to exist. Every group had a different dynamic based on the people involved in it. Ranging across different age groups, the experiences shared were applauded, fears validated, new friends made, help extended and so much more. These sessions didn't just end after three hours. They lingered on for days in our heads, sometimes even weeks.

As gratifying as it is to have a bunch of people come together and share experiences, I also wanted to make professional services accessible to all. Basic rights, for instance, are often misinterpreted. We tend to believe a lot of things we read on the internet which might not be correct. Whether married or divorced, it's good to know your rights. I invited a bunch of experts to come and speak to the participants and address any common doubts. Since these were larger sessions, it wasn't necessary to limit the number of attendees. We had 100+ participants for almost every session conducted. For those interested in taking it further one-on-one, they could always reach out to the experts. Professionals from three important related fields of work were invited to conduct these sessions.

1. Lawyers: These are the most important professionals required when you decide to divorce. The focus was on learning about basic rights, how to choose the

right lawyer for yourself, what are the different types of petitions you can file, how alimony works, child custody battles, and so much more. A good lawyer can help you to get an overarching understanding of what it is like to be in court and how to prepare before court.

2. Therapists: Most divorces are taxing, and the stigma is even more so. To make healing a smooth and easy process, these sessions gave others a sneak peek into the benefits of therapy and how a professional could help. This was broken down with insights into how effective it could be in particularly stressful situations, seen through the lens of a divorce as well as the associated stigma. The best outcome was making therapy accessible while also untangling the complexities and reluctance that participants had.

3. Financial planning: These workshops were hosted only for women. It's well understood that a lot of women are stuck in marriages only because they're financially dependent on their partner and unfortunately cannot leave their house because of this. But is there a way we could plan our finances so that we're able to put away a small amount every month as an emergency fund in such situations? Can housewives find hobbies that could pay them? Where to invest, how to invest and be smart with money and more was covered in these sessions.

Equipping yourself with the right information is a very empowering move. Knowing what rights you can exercise, whom you need to speak to, what the process is, and where you can find help gives you the confidence to take that giant step forward and find your freedom, if that's what you're looking for. A lot of the women I spoke to told me that they started deriving confidence from the time they started understanding processes better and planning a rough road map in their heads. I related to that as well. Arming yourself with ample information helps you propel your case forward with a lot more confidence.

One major drawback I noticed while holding online sessions was that I became the driving force of the group, as an individual. It also meant that during a session, only a limited number of people could be accommodated. My goal was to expand, and I also wanted the group to become more community led, rather than something that I directed. After a lot of input from those who previously attended these support sessions, I shifted the group to Telegram—a live chat support system that's always readily available to you. This meant that someone needing help any time round the clock could find what they were looking for. It also meant that anybody could take the lead to provide help.

I started the group and announced it online, and as of today, we're around 600+ members strong. The group has seen so many people finding strength through conversations that are thought-provoking, informative and supportive. Whether it's 4 p.m. or 2 a.m., there's always someone available to help, advise or mostly, just listen.

The group's aim was to provide ample support to those undergoing divorce (or those who have finished the process of divorce) to know that they're never alone. But what truly amazed me is how it beautifully branched out into so many avenues. Smaller groups found their way based on cities, and meet-ups were planned in Mumbai, Delhi, Chennai and Bangalore to name a few. This shifted the onus away from me and gave me the chance to sit back and let the community determine the way forward. Every time I receive photos of groups of people meeting, my heart swells with pride. Why, it even went international!

When a member posted on the group about wanting to restart her career to become financially independent after many years, the group members jumped to her aid to provide leads and introductions to their companies, and did whatever they could to make her transition into work life easier. But that wasn't an isolated event. Multiple times we witnessed the group members helping each other out. Recently, a dating channel has been set up as well, so the singles on the group get a chance to put themselves out there and find potential matches within the group itself.

This is the power of community. When people come together, magic happens. What started off as a safe space for support, soon diversified, and will continue to find so many more variations in different forms. Ultimately, the aim has been singular—to help those who need it.

If you find yourself in a situation where your marriage is ending and you don't know where to begin, try this. Take two steps back and try to detach *some* emotion from it so you can think practically for a few minutes. 'Some' being the keyword here, because I know how difficult it is to detach emotion from a process as gruelling as a divorce, but hey, when the going gets tough, the tough truly get going. Sprinkling practicality into an ocean of emotions might help you set sail towards the destination of your choice. Note down the first couple of actions you need to carry out. It's possible you can't entirely block out the emotion, but the more practically you're able to train yourself, the less emotionally drained you tend to feel.

Just remember—you've got this! And when you need it, we've got you.

Single Parenting

The impact, difficulty and repercussions of divorce increase dramatically when kids are involved in a marriage. The relationship is not only about the couple in these cases. The needs of the child must be taken into consideration as well. The age of the child, the help available, financial background, etc., play a pivotal role in making a decision as life-changing as a divorce. In most custody battles, the mother is given preference for primary custody, especially if the child is below the age of five. In India, the Guardian and Wards Act 1890 has drafted provisions for children and minors after divorce, which then branches out into different laws depending on the religion (Hindu/Muslim/Christian/Parsi Act).

Society also works in strange ways. In the 140+ interviews I conducted for this book, at least eighty have told me they've been given this one piece of advice on how to fix their marriage: 'Have a baby, everything will be all right.'

No, it will not make things right. Bringing a third person into a relationship that's not working between two people is only going to complicate things. It's the worst advice that a distressed couple could receive. Unfortunately, given how deeply influential families can be, many couples go ahead and procreate in the hope that the arrival of a baby will put an end to their troubles, or at the very least, distract them. In the long run, nobody wins in these situations, especially not the child or children brought into an already unhappy relationship.

Tejasvita, a therapist by profession, also told me, 'A baby's cortisol levels are higher when there's conflict at home. It's a common misconception that babies know nothing and it's just sad. There is a deep impact on everybody around when there's a bad relationship around. Did you know that an unhappy relationship could potentially lower life expectancy and also cause health problems?' She explains that her clients with kids find it much tougher to deal with marital strife than those without, and rightly so. Children are highly impressionable.

We've often heard the term 'broken home', meaning that a person comes from a divorced household. Can't a parent and a child be a complete, intact family if they choose to be? Being called 'broken' is something single parents are challenging strongly, through posts and blogs. By contrast, there's a sense of a 'complete' family when it's conventionally blessed by society. When a couple chooses to separate, it goes against societal norms, and unfortunately gets labelled 'broken'. A lot of single mothers have proudly written about the fact that their children live better lives with a single parent compared to being forced to live in a house where the parents aren't getting along, or even worse, in a house of abuse. 'What are we teaching our girls if mothers stay in homes where they're beaten up by the husband? We're telling them that that's how women are treated in marriages. And the sons? They learn that it's all right to beat your wife up when you're angry,' one mother said during one of the support group sessions. 'We need to teach our children better. I didn't want my daughter to grow up and believe that this is how marriages work. If she chooses to get married in the future, I'd like for her to know how to stand up for herself in any situation and be brave like her mother,' another single mom wonderfully chimed in.

In fact, the UN Women Annual Report 2019–2020 suggests an estimated 4.5 per cent of Indian households are being run by single women. Which is 13 million households! We even have celebrity single mothers in India who have proudly walked the red carpet with their children, including the likes of Sushmita Sen, Neena Gupta, Pooja Bedi, Ekta Kapoor and so on.

Many custody cases are emotionally taxing and can extend for long periods of time, especially when contested. However, there are also many couples who split amicably and share custody and finances, as well as continue to co-parent harmoniously. Physical, mental and financial health is extremely important for a single parent, particularly for a mother. While there are so many stories, each vastly different from the other, I bring to you some inspiring, heartbreaking, heart-warming stories from single parents who are bringing up children with so much sensitivity and sensibility. I don't have a child of my own, and all I could offer was my sympathy and support to the single parents I spoke to. I learnt a lot and thoroughly enjoyed each of these conversations, and I'm sure you will too.

'If you divorce him, then finally me and my sister will also get rid of him, Mamma. If you don't divorce him, then we're also stuck with him forever,' said Yana's elder daughter. Yana, who had just turned fifty-one, has two daughters who had been by her side all their lives, both in their twenties now. The three of them were a family. Their father lived in the same house but he had little to do with them. Yana and her husband were related and had an arranged marriage when she was twenty-two years old and her husband, thirty-two. It is common practice in the south of the country to marry within the family. At twenty-two, Yana didn't have much of a say in the marriage. She was raised by a single dad who was the centre of her universe, and she agreed to what he chose for her.

The problems in her marital life started very soon after her wedding. Her husband quit his job, for reasons still unknown to her. He flitted from job to job aimlessly, hiding many things from his family and being extremely secretive. Not only did this make Yana uneasy, it also led to a lot of financial instability for her family. A few years into her marriage, unfortunately her father passed away, leaving Yana utterly shattered. Being the only daughter, she inherited his property, which her husband pressured her to move in to very quickly. Here's where financial abuse became more prevalent in her life. Yana soon converted her dad's garage into an office space and started her own private practice as a doctor. Her credentials and hard work meant she became the sole breadwinner for the family. Under severe stress and pressure from her husband, who claimed he was starting his own business, she had to sell her jewellery and even her father's house. The proceeds from these sales have since gone missing. The business never took off and she received no returns. All this time, Yana raised her two daughters on her own. 'My father was the man I saw growing up, so somewhere I just assumed that my husband will also be a very responsible man towards his family, but I was in for a rude shock. As a woman, I was expected to respect my husband only because of age. I mean, how stupid?' Yana quips angrily.

I asked her how she inched closer towards wanting a divorce, and she explained to me how she waited until her younger daughter turned eighteen. Even if one of them, at any point, had resisted the divorce, she wouldn't have gone through with it. Her daughters had seen enough growing up and only wanted their mom to get her freedom. One day when her husband was at home, Yana begged him to give her a divorce and leave them alone. He reluctantly agreed. They went to court once and were asked to come back in six months (as per mutual consent norms) to sign the final papers. After the initial court appearance, Yana's husband absconded. Along with her lawyer, till date, she's sent him over twenty notices asking him to appear. His absence has forced Yana to withdraw the mutual consent petition and file a fresh contested divorce petition against her husband. So many relatives, including his mother, have shunned Yana and her daughters and have refused to reveal his whereabouts to them. When other relatives came to know of her situation, she faced her fair share of stigma as well. 'If the children are young, they comment on why you'd do that to young children. If the children are older, then that's a problem too. What *is* the correct age that one can even leave their husband?' she smiled painfully. 'I'm fifty-one and I'm not expected to have sexual urges either. I'm considered too old.' But she adds that the toughest part of the stigma she faces is how she'll manage to get her daughters married if she chooses to divorce their father. She's lost money, a marriage and a lot of self-respect through this thirty-year ordeal.

Her court experience was quite demeaning as well. As she stood in the witness box, she faced censure from the judge, who didn't believe her husband had absconded. 'Call him now on your phone,' she demanded. As she'd predicted, her husband did not answer her call. The judge still didn't believe her. 'Call him via Truecaller so I know you're calling the right person,' she told Yana. Her lawyer offered to call via the app. It was the right number and there was no answer. It has taken a lot of effort for Yana and her lawyer to fight this case, and she is still in court waiting for her missing husband to come forward and finish the divorce. With two beautiful daughters by her side, I'm rooting for Yana to find her freedom very soon.

On the other hand, when Firoza and her husband separated, she sat her seven-year-old son down and walked him through the change in their lives. 'Eleven years of marriage and a seven-year-old child later, a divorce is painful,' says the highly successful divorce lawyer from Mumbai. She armed herself with books like *Dinosaurs Divorce: A Guide for Changing Families* and *Two Homes*— both of which have been written keeping kids in mind, to help them think of divorce as a positive outcome for their families. 'Our partnership is over, but our parenting is forever,' Firoza added. Showing empathy towards each other during a separation is very taxing, but as parents, they did their best to ensure a smooth transition for their son. They introduced him to two homes, one for each parent, along with the idea that both the homes are happy homes that are his. It also took a lot of constant reassurance that their son is loved equally, by both parents. 'Big people also have problems. Not all marriages end in divorce though. There are people who can make it work and people who cannot make it work,' she told her son, citing the example of his grandparents, who have made their marriage work for many years now. With time, Firoza's constant communication and effort paid off, and her son has accepted their family situation rather smoothly.

One of the biggest challenges for single parents is missing the support of the other parent when things get difficult. Tough days are a regular occurrence for any parent.

But single parents manage by falling back on their strong support system of friends, family and others—friends who can babysit, grandparents who can entertain a child for a whole weekend, and other single parents who keep them company in this journey. All this enables them to take a break, indulge in some self-care, and to be the best version of themselves. They say it takes a village to raise a kid, and that is more true for single parents.

Meenakshi was already a famous artist when her son was born. She wasn't a single parent then. She got married for the second time to a wonderful man who was also getting married for the second time. As their son grew up and was old enough to understand, Meenakshi took the time to explain to him that this wasn't the first time she was married, that her past had no bearing on who she is currently, and that they are a family now. The same applied to his father as well. The son's questions were answered and the two divorces in the family are behind them, never to be brought up or discussed again—not because there's anything to hide, but because they're not relevant any more.

After seventeen years of marriage, forty-six-year-old Nitin and his wife called it quits. They have two children, aged twenty and eighteen now. Four years into their marriage, they knew it wasn't working. They found they were not compatible but mutually decided to live under the same roof in separate rooms, for the sake of their son and daughter. 'Once you are parents, you need to think of your kids first,' Nitin said, and went on to add, 'my ex-wife is a wonderful person, no doubt there. But we just weren't getting along.' We're also conditioned to believe that this is how marriages work—arguments and unhappiness are normalized as something we have to accept as part of the package. 'If we'd gotten/reached out for help at the right time, our problems wouldn't have intensified as much as they actually did,' Nitin says. He finds it extremely unfair that in this country so much is swept under the carpet, allowing issues to fester and grow. I asked him if he regrets staying in the marriage only for the sake of his kids and he let out a reluctant, 'Maybe we should have divorced earlier,' and smiled. As the kids grew older, talks of separation were gradually introduced to them. His daughter, like many young girls, discussed it with her friends at school. Fortunately for kids these days, divorce isn't as alien a word as it was even twenty years ago. The kids had friends in class whose parents were divorced, and so they knew what it meant. So, when Nitin's daughter opened up to her friends, she wasn't worried about judgement. In fact, she received support from her friends' parents as well. As Nitin's kids grew older and fully grasped the situation, they started to feel guilty as their parents stayed together only for them, not because they wanted a partnership. The separation, however, didn't go as planned. A heated argument led to Nitin's ex-wife packing her bags and moving temporarily to her friend's house. It wasn't the ideal way to tell their kids but sometimes things don't go according to plan. They eventually opted for a mutual consent divorce, with some complications over alimony. They also decided on shared custody of their children, with the mother getting primary custody. The children stay with Nitin two days a week. It has now been two years since the divorce and he tells me that co-parenting has been a learning experience. But it has also been a challenge to remain civil and not get into further fights. It's the children who are more understanding and help control the situation to the best of their ability. In fact, his daughter shares memes with her father that mock divorced parents, and the two bond through laughing at them.

One of the most important points that Nitin brought up touched me extremely deeply. He mentioned how devastated he was immediately after the separation. He knew it was only a matter of time, but when he actually had to move out of his house and into an empty apartment, it hit him like a ton of bricks. Having grown up in a bustling home with siblings, and then as part of a family with two kids, he suddenly found himself alone, and he wasn't prepared for that. 'I did want companionship and I created a profile on dating apps. But it was truly the worst of the worst experiences. It gave me so much more anxiety than the divorce,' he said, shaking his head vigorously. His counsellor told him that usually men react very differently to a divorce than women.

A woman knows what it's like to be uprooted from her home as soon as she gets married. A man doesn't.

Men usually have it easier than women. It's only during a divorce that they realize what it means to be completely displaced from a familiar environment. Women leave their parents' house with its sense of belonging and familiarity, and move in with a new family. They learn to adapt and adjust to a new environment, new traditions and new ways of life. Women are told from an early age that one day they'll leave their parents to live with their husband. It's what girls are taught to do. But it's different for boys, who are taught that they will bring a bahu (daughter-in-law) home. After a couple gets married, it's always the woman who's 'given away' to another family, completely unrooting herself and adjusting to a whole new dynamic. It's what's been happening for generations. While it's anecdotal rather than based on scientific evidence, women tend to stay calmer during a divorce than men.

As time rolled by, Nitin found companionship, and today he's in a loving, happy and healthy relationship with a woman who has a history of divorce as well. He took a year to gauge the stability of this relationship before introducing his partner to his children and parents. They're on great terms today and even take vacations together!

Nandini Raman, a counsellor and therapist who works not just with couples but also their children when required, sat down with me to explain how divorce affects various age groups of children in different ways. The age group between twelve and fifteen are in a transitional phase, and this may affect their reaction to divorce. Children below ten years old are usually more unpredictable since they might not understand what is happening. What's important in any divorce case is that both parents need to have a very clearly defined role in the children's life and stick to that as far as possible. Some children might express their anger.

Some might be accepting. Some might just go silent. Whatever the case may be, it is important to ensure that communication is always strong between the parents and the child.

'My son and my fiancé are just . . . best friends,' Kaashvi beamed. Her wedding was coming up in less than ten days, and she was all smiles, blushes and joy. Kaashvi called it quits with her ex-husband many years ago when her son was about a year old. Her parents refused to accept the decision, especially after she birthed a child. They forced her to go back to her husband with whom she spent another two years, feeling lost, isolated and fed up. One fine day, she found the courage to walk out again, but this time, with a lot more conviction. It was a mutual split this time around, and Kaashvi managed to find a cosy home in the same locality. Luckily, her parents lived nearby as well. To help her five-year-old boy settle in, she first moved in with her parents, since the grandparents were her boy's favourites. Slowly, she set up her house and started to bring him over once or twice a week. He gradually became familiar with the house, and finally, they moved in together full time. Her son continued to visit his father and spend time with him on weekends. He did ask Kaashvi questions about why they weren't in their previous house, why his dad lived elsewhere, and when they would live together as a family. Kaashvi, who had fully prepared herself for these exact questions, sat him down and explained that his parents were fighting and not getting along, which meant that although they will be friends in the future, they wouldn't be living together.

'That hurts me, Amma, please don't say that,' he told her one day, breaking down. Kaashvi was heartbroken but she knew she needed to take responsibility for her decisions and felt it was important that she explained to her son. She did just that. She always kept the lines of communication open and answered every question as honestly as she could. Like many good things that take time, almost two years after she moved out of her husband's home, her son has made peace with their new life.

An Instagram DM found Kaashvi a new love in her life. 'I wasn't ready for a relationship at all back then but you know how it is!' she blushed. Her divorce hadn't fully come through when Kaashvi met her new friend. Soon enough, they both knew it was more than a friendship. In this case, there was a lot more than just herself to consider—any new relationship had to involve her son as well. Although her boyfriend lives abroad, Kaashvi ensured she found a way for him to spend time with her son and gave them the space to bond. Their love story is heart-warming. Her son and partner got along extremely well, putting Kaashvi at ease with the relationship—enough for her to even consider tying the knot again. 'It isn't easy, a lot of past triggers affect me till date, but I'm so glad to have a fiancé who communicates extremely well and is wonderfully patient with me,' she adds. I asked her how his family dealt with the idea of him marrying a divorced woman with a five-year-old son, and she told me that it was up to her fiancé to convince them. The family, however, posed no problem. Their only concern was whether their son was ready to start parenting a five-year-old, but he was up for the challenge. Kaashvi was giddily excited, planning her wedding, which is going to be a small and intimate affair at a temple far away from the city. Kaashvi's is a story of hope I am going to revisit, and I'm sure you are too, for many months to come!

Some single parents have it much tougher than others. While speaking to Roja, I was on the verge of tears as she described the hardships she was facing. After suffering abuse from her husband, she's still running pillar to post in different courts fighting for her divorce. Her two-year-old daughter, who is suffering from a speech impediment and also falls in the autism spectrum, takes up a lot of Roja's time and attention, and rightly so. Roja shifted to a part-time job to be able to better tend to her daughter's needs, which has put a major strain on her financially. Roja lives with her parents and receives moderate support from them. It's not easy for them either. Her husband has relinquished all rights to his daughter, and Roja currently has full custody of her child. Because her husband wants nothing to do with his child, Roja plunges into eternal confusion and frustration about how to complete school forms—whose name she should put in the father column, what she should change her child's surname to, and how she can erase him from her daughter's life. It's not easy on her, and her anxiety is seen in the way her eyebrows waver into a frown as she talks about the torment her husband is putting her through.

Sita was a bit of a rebel in her early twenties, for she fell in love with someone whom her parents vehemently

rejected and then ran away from home in an attempt to
marry him. She was all of twenty years old then. Somehow,
her parents managed to bring her back to their home,
and they quickly got her married to a stranger through an
arranged marriage. Sita was lost and heartbroken, and it
took her a while to understand the whirlwind of change
around her. Today, nineteen years later, Sita is divorced
and lives with her seventeen-year-old son alone in a big
city. The divorce wasn't easy. The marriage was complex
because it was loveless. It didn't help that there was little
or no effort from her ex-husband as well. Eventually, even
though her parents disapproved again, Sita went ahead and
did what was best for her and her son. To his credit, her son
was extremely supportive of her decision and has chosen
to stay with her. Following her divorce, it was difficult to
find a house as a single mother with a teenage son, and
it was only through known contacts that she managed to
find a place to live. 'I didn't want to lie to any landlord.
I told them the truth, that I'm a single parent and yes, I
will have friends and family who will visit,' Sita said. My
favourite twist to this story is that she reconnected with
her previous lover after her divorce ended, and the two are
currently trying to make it work, almost twenty years later.
Talk about a story straight out of a fantasy novel!

While speaking to Zara and her fiancé, Manav, I
was really intrigued by the story they narrated of meeting
Manav's parents. Zara has an eight-year-old daughter,
who Manav adores and treats as his own. When the couple
decided to tell his parents about their relationship, Manav

and Zara decided not to inform them of Zara's daughter. He first introduced them to Zara—a fun-loving, bubbly, Murakami fan. Considering Manav's dad was an avid reader himself, the two of them found they had much in common and easily slipped into smooth conversation. Manav's parents enjoyed Zara's company in the coming weeks, and it was only later that he told them about Zara's daughter. By this time, it wasn't defining who Zara was to them—they had already warmed up to her. Manav felt that speaking about Zara's daughter at the very beginning would have set the tone differently, and he was worried that his parents would only focus only on that point, forgetting that Zara was an individual in her own right, and her identity extended to something more than being a mother. Considering his parents already really liked Zara, meeting her daughter and accepting her became a lot simpler for everybody involved. This is a technique I've heard quite a few couples use to introduce their partner who has a child, and if you think it might help in your case, you could adopt it too!

During one in-person support group, I recall an incident that brought everyone in the group closer together. A mother had attended the session, and while introducing herself, she spoke about how she'd lost custody of her daughter to her husband. She was feeling immense guilt. She burst into tears, and shared with us how isolated and lonely she felt. She was also questioning her ability as a parent, she recalled her pregnancy phase, and she told us just how much she loves her little girl. The group stood up in unison to hug her, pass on their strength and remind her that the fight isn't over. The energy was infectious. We could see she was feeling better and the life was returning to her face as she promised to continue fighting. Other women shared phone numbers with her and urged her to keep in touch when she needed to find her strength again. Ah, community.

Single parents are true rock stars. To make a decision to end a marriage while also keeping in mind their child or children and their entire future, is a bigger deal. Every single parent I spoke to showed immense grit, determination, courage and equal part vulnerability.

Children of Divorce

'I will never choose to divorce because the blame will shift on my mother, who divorced my father,' Ria says. She's not in an unhappy marriage at the moment, but she needs to consider the option hypothetically because of the traumatizing and extremely difficult events that have led to her feeling this way. When Ria was all of six years old, she saw her father assaulting her mother in the kitchen. Terrified, she ran to an aunty in the neighbourhood, yelling for help. In response, she was asked to 'quickly stop the fight'. A petite, tiny tot was asked to 'stop' a well-built, grown man whose anger she feared the most. How in the world was she expected to stop it from happening? As she grew up, it only got worse. Physical abuse led to emotional abuse, which also led to social abuse, where her father would cuss at her mother publicly, and had no qualms about insulting her in front of friends and family. 'He was just a really terrible, vile human,' Ria recounts.

She'd just turned nineteen when her parents got a divorce. They'd been separated for a long time and it was no surprise to anyone. Her father didn't even turn up for the proceedings and they were granted an *ex parte* divorce. When Ria's parents finally got the divorce, it was a huge relief. 'It also felt like a divorce between father and daughter, you know? He's divorcing any rights on me as well,' Ria said. She added that there was no love lost, so it didn't matter. Ria and her younger sibling were a team against him, fiercely protecting their precious mother from him.

When Ria moved out of her home for further studies, she found it more convenient to tell acquaintances that her parents were 'estranged'. It became her favourite word. Separated or divorced felt too real and legal, whereas estranged made a different impression. It was an easy way to escape the stigma, at least temporarily. For a long time, others told her that her face tells a story of some sadness in her life. She didn't even realize how much trauma she was unconsciously carrying with her everywhere she went. It's been such a long time. Ria is now thirty-four but she still remembers being terrified of her father's eyes widening when he was ready to strike or him grinding his teeth in seething anger. It is still a trigger for her, which she is working through with the help of therapy.

As Ria scaled up her career and started to meet more people, she sometimes found herself telling people that her father was dead. It was an easier choice than saying the word divorce.

A dead parent brought her sympathy but divorce brought her judgement.

Ria says she has managed to fine-tune her coping mechanisms with age and time. 'But what's truly the hardest part of this is when I see another girl really loved by her father. It really hits me then that I didn't have that chance, and never will again. I deserved it as a child, and I was robbed of it,' Ria sighs.

When Ria fell in love and got married, her in-laws were extremely understanding and sensitive to her situation. They even printed an invitation that invited guests to their 'daughter-in-law and son's reception', without hurting anyone's sentiments. They also ensured that nobody asked any unsolicited questions. Ria didn't notice till much later and was full of gratitude when she found out. It was a small, silent gesture of support, and not many understand how well it shielded her. She refused to invite her father to her wedding, much to the dismay of her relatives. He had only harmed her family, hurt her mother, and made Ria and her brother feel unloved. What right did he have to be a part of celebrating her wedding after so many years of being apart? Yes, he's her biological father, but logically, it made no sense for him to be there. She even wrote about this on her social profiles, to let it be known openly.

A few years before her wedding, she found out via Facebook that her father had remarried. The news brought up a lot of trauma and anger that still affects her today. Ria's mother's life was completely ruined. She went from marriage to kids to divorce, existing only to feed her children and ensure a decent education for the two of them. Her father, who got out of a marriage he abused and used for his convenience, never assumed the responsibility of taking care of his kids, not even financially, restarted his life with someone new and moved on, leaving her mother stuck in the same house and riddled with stigma that meant she never had a chance to find another companion. She continues to completely dedicate her life to her children, and that's the reality for many single mothers in the country who got divorced over two decades ago.

I also got the chance to meet sweet little Mishika, who took time out from her busy play date with friends to quickly speak to me. All of nine years old, Mishika's clarity of thought and understanding astounded me. Her parents, who had recently been divorced amicably, clearly communicated with her and assuaged her doubts. I asked her what she felt and understood about her parents' situation, and she said, 'Well, I really like going to Dad's house over the weekends and staying at Mom's house on the weekdays. Even my friends like my dad's house. My mom told me last week that she's really happy.' It was extremely refreshing and adorable to observe her nuanced understanding of the situation. I also asked her if she discussed it with her friends and she said she did. She explained to them that her parents are friends and that her family is still a family. Mishika's parents are learning to co-parent and keep the atmosphere joyful. I asked Mishika's mother if she's open to dating or remarrying, and she answered in the affirmative. It's an open field to play in right now, and she's very much ready to welcome any possibility in the future.

'I lost my childhood very early to my parents' divorce,' Ivaan's voice breaks and he tries to hold it together as he walks back in time to when he was about seven years old. Hiding behind shelves and sofas, Ivaan has seen his parents have terrible fights and even seen his father violently hit his mother. As a young kid, when one is exposed to such an environment, it has long-term effects. One fine day, when his mother couldn't take any more abuse, she wrote a letter saying she was leaving the house and moved out, leaving Ivaan with his father. At his young age, Ivaan couldn't comprehend what was happening or even know what questions to ask. It took another seven months before they were able to establish contact again with his mother. Reconciliation efforts were made but proved futile, leading to his parents' divorce. His father took custody of him and they continued to live in the same house as before. For about a year after their divorce, he would meet his mother every once in a while, but she would suddenly disappear and there would be no communication for long periods of time. This catapulted Ivaan into a lot of confusion. It came as a huge shock to Ivaan and his father when his mother remarried, because she had never mentioned this to them. The next time Ivaan saw her was in court, where his father was clashing with his mom since she'd filed for custody of Ivaan, following her new marriage. Ivaan was asked to tell the judge where he wanted to live. When he appeared in front of the judge, Ivaan chose his father as the parent he wanted to grow up with. This closed the case. For reasons unknown to Ivaan, his mother sadly passed away a couple of years later. Before she fell ill, her second marriage had also failed. Ivaan breaks down when he speaks of the deep regret he carries for not being by his mother's side during her last days, or even being able to perform her last rites as the only son. He was too young back then to be able to make constructive, well-thought-out decisions, and he didn't have a great support system to fall back on either. The trauma from his childhood made him highly introverted, which made it difficult for him to cultivate friendships. He's had two friends all his life, and when he meets someone new, he's unable to talk about his parents' divorce.

Ivaan started questioning marriage during his teenage years, since all he had seen was a 'broken home', tears, trauma and a lost parent. He didn't believe the institution would bear any fruits for him. But this changed when one of his two friends ended up falling in love with him. Today, they're happily married with a three-year-old boy they're raising together in the city. He is in a very happy marriage that has changed his beliefs, but his regret over not having done more for his mother runs extremely deep. He says it is something he possibly won't ever be able to make peace with.

Kids probably have the strongest reactions, like the lyrics of the famous song by Savage Garden say, 'animals and children tell the truth, they cannot lie'. It is mind-boggling that the advice of having a child to solve marital problems is so common without a single thought of the impact it will have on the child that will be brought into this world. Some parents have a knack of figuring out the mess, and some don't, leaving their children in a mess. The ripple effect is felt not just in everyday lives, but especially when these children grow up and have relationships and marriages of their own. As decades roll by, this becomes a compounded issue that later feels too big to address. Having said that, I should also appreciate the parents who've truly figured it out for themselves, raising children who grow up with evolved thoughts and understanding of how it's perfectly all right for parents to lead different lives.

If you're a child of divorce, or a parent whose child has witnessed a divorce, here's a big hug to you.

Hope after Divorce

If you've read this far, first, thank you. Second, the good part is just beginning. We now know about stigma, the difficulties in court and facing society. But we also need to know about life after a divorce, right? About falling in love again and finding a partner who makes you feel equal, loved and respected. Or perhaps remaining single and completely enjoying life. Stick around, friend. These stories are going to warm your heart, for there's so much to look forward to, and so much love in this world waiting to be absorbed and enjoyed.

Hope after divorce can manifest itself in so many ways. The most hopeful part when we speak about life after divorce is that you get to define what it means for you. I remember one feisty friend giving me this pep talk before I got divorced, 'Nobody gives a f*ck about you after you get divorced. At least for a while. That will be your time to shine. Society gives up on you. Nobody asks you anything because it's too damn awkward, and trust me, you'll literally be breathing fresh air.' It made me chuckle back then, and now I know that she was absolutely right. Hope after divorce could be finally discovering (or rediscovering) yourself, travelling alone, taking up that hobby you always wanted to pursue, connecting more with your friends, exploring new concepts, falling in love again, shifting gears in your career, moving to a new location, living by yourself for the first time ever, adopting a kid, learning a new life skill, challenging yourself, or so many other things. Marriage needn't be the ultimate destination in your life. You're currently standing at the edge of the cliff, screaming with joy that you're free to fly.

I asked friends, acquaintances and strangers who are divorced what hope after the divorce meant for them, and I got such a vast variety of responses. For the romantic at heart, some of these stories might make you weep. Brace yourselves.

A divorce can potentially set someone back a few years in terms of growth but when they bounce back, it is with a new rigour, maturity, learning, acceptance and deeper clarity. The glow up is very real! It's true for me and it's true for many others as well. An unhappy marriage, coping at court, facing society afterwards—these things may not kill you but they definitely make you stronger. They make your heart wiser and your head bolder.

After my divorce, I didn't want the thought of companionship, love, romance or even marriage to change for the worse because of one bad experience. I wanted to give it time, enjoy my new-found singledom and keep myself open to any possibility in the future. I wasn't going to allow one experience to put a dampener on future prospects. Not surprisingly, I found a lot of other women agreeing with my thoughts on this. It's beautiful how love wins over hate most of the time.

One incident stands out for me because it makes me laugh even today. I matched with a guy on a dating app and we got talking. It was a fairly interesting conversation filled with puns, TV show references and some song lyrics as well. I had not mentioned 'divorced' on my profile back then, so it's possible he had stumbled upon me on some social platform. I hadn't heard from him for a few days when he texted me saying, 'Hey. I've had a great time talking to you. But I've found out that you're divorced and my mother will not approve of you. So, unmatching you. Take care.' I'm copying the text verbatim here. I was dumbfounded when I read it at first, but then I sent a screenshot of it to my girlfriends and we had a good laugh about it. I narrate this story so many times because it never ceases to amuse me.

But like I said, I never gave up on the idea of falling in love. It's beautiful to find someone to share life with. As much as I enjoyed every minute of finding myself in my single days, I always knew I ultimately wanted to find companionship—the gushing, sweet, butterflies-in-the-tummy, Mani Ratnam kind of love. It might not be Madhavan in a local train or Dulquer at a church wedding, but whatever it was, I was open to it. And I think the patient waiting was absolutely worth it. I met someone in

2021, on a dating app, who with time, changed the way I experienced love. It was easy, smooth and extremely reassuring. It continues to feel even better than a Mani Ratnam movie. I took my time after the divorce. I worked hard and invested in therapy, and it paid off. I've grown up in so many ways, and experience has been the best teacher. Venky and I connect emotionally on so many levels, our laugh is the loudest in most rooms, our communication skills are on point, we try to find new adventures, discover ourselves individually and together during travels, and mostly learn to love each other for who we are in the present, and not define ourselves by what the past has been. We're planning to tie the knot in 2024, and I often look back and marvel at how far I've come, remember the other stories of hope I held on to, and always tell myself that one day I'll be my own inspirational story. A divorce is a part of the story, but it has no bearing on what lies ahead. There's so much to look forward to in the future, and for that, I'm giddily excited.

My dear friend Nishita's story will inspire you as much as it did me. She had a typical arranged marriage that her family approved of—horoscopes perfectly matching and all that. Soon, she became a victim of abuse. She'd get beaten up, kicked and pushed. Like so many other women, she kept quiet about this and carried on with life, wondering if that was all marriage had to offer. When she found out she was pregnant, she hoped this would change the relationship between her and her then-husband. But when she was seven months pregnant, in the midst of a freezing cold winter, her husband abandoned her on a deserted highway after kicking her out of the car during an argument. This pushed her too far. 'You're better than this,' she kept repeating to herself. She soon birthed a beautiful baby boy, Yash, and moved back to India with him. Opening up to her family about the abuse she'd been through was the starting point of her path to freedom. A set of supportive parents can restore a woman's confidence. With a small baby in her arms, she bravely applied for a divorce. With therapy, solo trips, friends who lifted her up and a family that backed her, she started to find her feet. Nishita rebuilt her life and had many professional successes and promotions. It was time to ensure her personal life got its due as well. A few years down the line, as she was scrolling through Tinder, she found a profile that mentioned interest in history— something that deeply interested her too. She went on a few dates with Sri and knew without doubt that there was more to explore there. Sri soon met Nishita's son, who was almost seven years old now. They got along like a house on fire, which, as you might have guessed, was a fairly important criterion for Nishita. Exclusivity found its way into their relationship, which strengthened as each day passed. At first, it was only Sri and Yash who spent time together. Soon, Yash met Sri's other siblings, who couldn't stop raving about what a fun kid he is. Sri's parents became curious, and they had a desire to meet this special child. When they finally met, it was beautiful. Nishita says she felt extremely anxious before the meeting, but once conversation started flowing, she felt completely at ease.

When so many things aligned and clicked, it was inevitable that the families decided to take it further. They welcomed Yash and Nishita into their family wholeheartedly. One of the best events I have attended in my life is their wedding, in which I clearly remember Yash telling all the guests that he's getting a father and how they're now 'one big happy family'. I cried as I watched this child embrace his mother's choices so openly and beautifully. When I think of this family, I realize how much we, as a society, need more families and a love like Sri's—progressive, welcoming and respectful.

While dating apps work well for many, let's take a moment to talk about matrimony sites and apps and how they work. A few months ago, a popular matrimony site reached out to me for a promotion deal. They were opening a 'divorce matrimony' portal and wanted to spread the word about it. On the one hand, I was happy to see divorce taking up space and being centre stage. But on the other hand, I couldn't accept the platform either, and here's why. Opening up a separate portal as 'divorce matrimony' is a means of discrimination. Now you're divorced, so here's a chance to meet more divorced people. This basically goes against everything I'm trying to work towards. When we say divorce is normal, what does normal include? How am I different from a person who hasn't divorced before? Can I not find love with a person who didn't set foot in family court? Why is my value diminishing? Of course, let me make it extremely clear that I have no issues with two divorced people meeting each other and choosing to be partners. If they do, that's fantastic. I'm very clear in my stance: that as a divorced person, I should be included in a dating or matrimonial pool that's for all single people and not segregated into just a divorced segment. I explained this to the marketing team at the matrimony app company, and politely declined the offer.

In recent times, there was uproar on the internet against IITshaadi, which was a matrimonial portal only for those who went to certain select colleges. Twitterati called it unfair, irrational and discriminatory. I beg to ask, isn't that the same for divorce as well? Give us the option to add divorce on a regular matrimonial profile, as per our discretion. Make it a free choice, as opposed to making it my identity and therefore restricting me to one set of profiles.

In the case of Priya, she was insistent on marrying only another divorced person. She felt it was the only way another man would understand what she went through. She found what she was looking for and is now happily married for a second time. Rucha, on the other hand, didn't necessarily want a divorced person. She ventured into the dating world and met a sailor who swept her off her feet. He wasn't married before, and the fact that she was didn't matter to either of them. They each had a preference, made a choice, and went ahead with it. Proposing a 'divorce matrimony' site robs me, and other divorced people, of our choice. Empowering people with the agency to choose the kind of partners they want and letting each one decide for themselves truly defines what 'normal' means in this context—for you, for me, for the betterment of society. If you, along with me, accept divorce as normal, then you should also be accepting of marrying a divorced person as normally as a non-divorced person. It's not very complicated now, is it?

I'll stress the same point again—that it's not worthy of applause that a man would choose to marry a divorced woman. Applaud them for their decision together, and applaud them for choosing to put effort into a new relationship. Don't applaud him as a hero for choosing to 'give a second life' to a fallen woman. Statements such as these, more common than you can imagine them to be, are the reason divorced women feel they're a burden and aren't deserving of love again. I've heard of a family who put their son on a pedestal for marrying a divorced woman's daughter. Read that again. That's just another example of how far we can stoop as a society in making women feel less than they are.

Tahira's story of marrying for a second time blew me away. Three years after her divorce and a lot of soul-searching and healing later, she felt she might be open to dating. Guess who pushed her into it? Her mother! From worrying herself sick about Tahira's divorce and its repercussions, here was her mother urging her to date, even if it was without the intention to marry—to be open to meeting new men and put herself out there. Tahira, curious by nature, decided to open up a profile on a non-mainstream dating app to see what the crowd there was like. 'If I matched with someone there, the fact that we wanted something non-mainstream might itself be a point of connection,' she smirked. And how right she was! She found a profile that appealed to her: his smile, his interest in traditional Indian music, and his well-written bio. She showed it to her mom first and told her she was going to swipe right. Here's the catch: he was 1500 kilometres away, in a city she'd never set foot in. Harish swiped right on her too, and they ended up chatting regularly for over a month. It worried her that just speaking on the phone might not be definitive enough for her to know how much she liked him, and so she arranged a meeting at a location halfway between the two cities they lived in. Looking back, it always felt like it was meant to be, for both of them. He spoke Tamil, she spoke Hindi, he eats meat, she eats vegetables, they lived on almost opposite ends of the country and met once a year, but the connection and love saw them through their dating phase. She told him upfront about her divorce and only wanted to proceed if he made peace with it, and that included him telling his family about it. 'Once the honeymoon phase of the first three months wore out, my insecurities and trauma from my first marriage made it a challenge to be in the relationship,' Tahira recounts. Healing isn't linear. Even in a safe space with her new partner, she went through ups and downs and felt uneasy at times. It took several months of clear communication, patience and a lot of work to move the needle in their relationship so it felt stable.

What I found most interesting in her story was how Harish introduced her to his family. Harish had initially suggested creating a WhatsApp group with her and his sister, but Tahira resisted it since it felt like a very big step. Instead, Tahira followed his sister and his mother on Instagram and vice versa. While no conversation followed, they viewed each other's stories, reacted with emojis, and so on. So, there was a feeling of familiarity but they didn't really know each other. Harish's parents were probably curious about Tahira's divorce but Harish drew very clear boundaries on what they could know and how much they could ask. He wasn't married before and it didn't matter to him that Tahira once was. He requested his parents to maintain distance from the topic, and surprisingly, they obliged. Tahira also speculated that none of the questions reached her because Harish protected her from them and dealt with it himself, and rightfully so—they are his parents after all. After months of Instagram communication, when she met his parents, which incidentally happened to be the day of their engagement, they weren't strangers. Today, two months after their beautiful temple wedding, they live together with his family, peaceful and harmonious. I've truly taken a page out of Tahira's book, and I hope you can too.

This conversation segued into an interesting discussion with Tahira, as well as a few others. Tahira had to fight with her parents to allow her to marry her first husband. She faced resistance because of his caste and religion. This is very common in many Indian households—even today, inter-caste and inter-religion marriages face a lot of opposition. While there has been some progress, we have a long way to go before we can say we're a society that accepts all types of marriages. Tahira managed to get her way, got married, and eventually got divorced as well. When she met Harish, despite being from a different caste, religion, language, location, almost everything—there wasn't any opposition. 'All I want is a good husband for you,' her mother said. It is probably coming from a place of love, but in most cases, when parents are in the process of getting their daughters married a second, or even a third time, surprisingly, caste, religion, food and languages cease to matter. Having seen their children go to hell and back, many parents have been known to change the way they approach marriage the next time around. This time, they focus on happiness, a good family, values and acceptance. Tahira and I laughed and sighed at the same time at how many divorces could be avoided, 'If only parents used different filters for the first marriage itself.'

A common doubt that other divorced women have reached out to me about is whether they should mention they're divorced on their dating profile or if it would be misleading to leave it out. Are you seeing the level of shame women associate with divorce? Imagine feeling like you're misleading someone because you haven't mentioned upfront that you're divorced. For some, it might be necessary because it's an easy filter to weed out uninterested parties, but it definitely isn't something that's mandatory. Being divorced doesn't become part of your identity. It's also a private matter for a lot of folks. When people pose this question, I tell them to put the divorce option out there only if they wish to and not because of the concern that it'd be misleading. If they find a good match and conversation starts to flow, then bring it up one-on-one when they start to feel comfortable.

While Tahira took the route of finding an unconventional dating app that wasn't mainstream, Mesha chose a very popular one. After we met in court, we managed to sporadically keep in touch, and I reached out to her for this book. Her profile was up and ready the very day after her divorce. She was all set to conquer the world of dating with her flair and sass. She said she enjoyed the attention she received from the apps. 'It might sound superficial, but it really isn't. I was in a marriage that gave me so little, left me so broken, and my self-worth felt like nothing. I really needed this to prop myself up again and if that included some external validation from men, then why the hell not!' she quipped, with a twinkle in her eye. I spoke to her twice. Once in 2019, and again in 2022. In 2019, she had met different kinds of men, and she told me that the dating game wasn't as bad as she thought it would be. Yes, of course, a lot of sifting is required. Disregarding creeps is a must, but there were men out there with interesting profiles and fun stories to share. 'I've put it up on my profile that I'm divorced,' she said, for she felt she had nothing to hide. If a man wasn't able to wrap his head around it, then it was an easy filter for her as well. She didn't want anything serious then, so she dated to have fun, let loose and come back home feeling like the world was her oyster. She even made great friends along the way, who she regularly kept in touch with. Mesha was upfront about the fact that she wasn't looking for a long-term relationship so as to not mislead anyone, and this ensured less drama ensued. Mesha knew that this phase of hers will end some day, for eventually she did want a monogamous relationship and a stable partnership with someone who was worth the emotional investment. A few months later, she matched with a man who was all that and more. 'I'm smitten,' she told me as she chomped down her sixth momo of the evening, trying to hide the incessant blushing. At a time when she wasn't even looking for it, it found her. The conversations, the madness, the connection, the compatibility, the travels, the comfort, the food, the laughter, and now, the love. I asked her if her divorce bothered her current partner, who hasn't been married before, and she had the widest smile on her face when she uttered a loud no. They'd spoken at length about this, and he was very clear that her present mattered the most to him, not her past. She mentioned it was really important to her that he truly understood why she chose to opt out of her marriage, and he made her feel that her decision was heard, understood and validated. In fact, he's even told her that he doesn't intend to hide the fact that she's divorced from his extended family. He's ready to step up and face the challenges and consequences, all the while holding her hand and walking into a future together. They're currently in a fulfilling and happy relationship, with a capacious, open-ended future.

After two divorces that almost tore his family apart, Sumesh decided to not venture into love or marriage again, for it felt like a waste of time and energy to him. He's convinced he made the right decision for himself, and he has communicated the same to those who care about him. He's focused on giving all his attention to his art and putting it out for the world to see. It's fulfilling and satisfying, and he's not answerable to anybody. His infectious smile said it all!

Aadhavi walked out of a sexless marriage, in which she felt no romance or compatibility with her partner—one chosen by her parents. The time between meeting him and marrying him was so short, she had no time to understand if he was the right one for her. It was difficult for her conservative family to understand why she'd openly speak about her sex life, and they didn't think it was a valid reason for her to end her marriage. But Aadhavi displayed exemplary conviction that she wasn't going to settle for a relationship that did not make her happy. Through many rounds of therapy, she learnt how to communicate with her parents, brought her parents in for sessions as well, and finally got a divorce. She wasn't sure how to navigate the dating world but soon found her footing and enjoyed the attention she received. Recently, she found a great match, one with whom she not only shares great comfort but also someone whose interests and values align with hers, and she fell in love. 'He's a year younger, but displays great maturity in accepting who I am. I didn't want sympathy. I just wanted plain acceptance, and I got what I wanted, 'Aadhavi says, with so much hope in her voice. They've decided to tie the knot in a few months in a small, simple wedding. Aadhavi's parents wanted to clear the air with her partner's parents, to ensure that they really felt okay with her being divorced. Their reaction was a definite sixer! His parents were almost embarrassed that they were asking this question. 'All we care about is that our son and his partner are happy, everything else doesn't matter.' And that's how they've closed that chapter of Aadhavi's past. Beautiful, isn't it?

Hope after divorce needn't just be love, or a new partner. Hope is an abstract entity, which comes in many different forms. Yashi describes hope after divorce as 'freedom'. She's given up on the idea of marriage and has chosen not to go down that path again. The inspiring thing is that she did not stop there. She sat her parents down, explained it to them, and eventually even found acceptance. She's opened up her life to dating multiple men, without being confined to just one.

For Naina too, marriage isn't something she wants to ever try again. 'Even if I meet the best guy in the world, I'd just live-in. I'm not involving the government in my relationship again and most definitely not planning on standing in a family court another time,' she asserted with pride. Naina hopes to establish herself as a travel blogger and influencer, and get funded to visit different countries, experience new cultures, food and people, and to write and vlog about it. While speaking with me, she was planning her diving trip to Fiji, and she said she's more excited about packing for the trip than she ever was even for a single day in her marriage.

Aishi had similar thoughts. 'I want to make money, I want to fall in love, I want to be happy. I don't see myself walking down the aisle again,' she told me happily. In fact, she was just getting ready for a date as she quickly exchanged notes with me. Being a sales leader, her job is demanding and extremely rewarding. She truly believes that if she does fall in love some day, she doesn't need a marriage to validate it. She's not sure her family will accept her stance on this but she's come such a long way since her divorce that nothing can stop her from choosing a life that's liberating, joyful and with zero regrets.

The common thread in these three stories is that they define hope differently, on their own terms. Even from personal experience, the way I viewed life after divorce refreshed my take on how the world functioned and how I fit into this large space. When I shared this with many other women, we completely related to it. When that freedom hits you, it changes you. It's like that breath you take when you've been underwater for a while and then you resurface. It's freeing, it's breathing life into you, and it's easing you back into that normality that you missed, or sometimes craved. I don't take small things for granted any more, and I don't make big changes without thinking them through. Similarly, for women like Yashi, Naina, Aishi and so many more who believe the same thing, marriage isn't the only option that inspires hope. So, if you're reading this, please believe that you aren't alone if you decide you don't want to get married again. It's a choice, after all. If being single and free is making you happy, then why not? Choose what's best for you, because you only live once. Yashi, Naina, Aishi and so many others will back you up—gladly.

'Twice divorced, and now married for a third time,' Anya gleamed. She first got married at the ripe age of nineteen, to a man who was twenty-five. Looking back, Anya recalls so many red flags she ignored, purely owing to age, and not knowing who she was and what she wanted. She let her emotions override all logic. But of course, back then, she did exactly what she wanted. Within a year, she faced emotional as well as physical abuse. 'My parents draw a line at abuse. I just wanted to get out of that marriage.' Anya was divorced by twenty-two. A romantic at heart, she found love again about three years later. 'I guess I felt like it was what was expected of me. I had to tick a few boxes and I did just that.' The man she married had to convince his parents about marrying someone who'd been divorced before, and while he did that, Anya had associated a lot of shame to it. It was mostly in her head but it lived up there rent-free. 'There's societal conditioning of expecting us to play certain roles and meet expectations. I don't know if I'm made to live up to them. I can't fit into the mould of gender-based roles either,' she said. As time passed, she evolved rather differently from her ex-husband, and it took a toll on their marriage. 'Looking back, I feel so stupid about the decisions I made in my twenties. Most of them are so regrettable. It's tough how so many young women in their twenties are expected to make such big life decisions, when they barely even have figured out who they are,' Anya, now thirty-eight, exclaims. The confidence, clarity and wonderfully crafted thoughts she has today come out in every single statement she makes. She divorced a second time in her twenties and wanted to be free and live life on her own terms. Of course, she faced harsh comments and stigma from relatives and even friends, but she and her parents had made up their mind to not let it affect them.

A decade full of healing, thinking, learning and unlearning later, she met a man who changed her life. It was during the pandemic, the unforgettable year of 2020, as she was scrolling through a dating app and came across a connection that grabbed her attention immediately. 'It's quite rare to see an Indian man not care about a woman with two divorces. He questioned how it's different from being in relationships. I agreed with him, but society doesn't, right?' she broke into laughter. Anya had also spent the last three years learning that divorce isn't bad, and by extension, she isn't bad because she's been through two divorces. You cannot stop a romantic at heart. Anya knew what she wanted and she got it. She's truly shattering stigma by openly speaking about her divorce and her current marriage. She has learnt not to let society dictate how she should live. Speaking to Anya felt like a beacon of hope that comfortably nestled into me.

For a lot of women, a second divorce seems like a lot. I heard someone at a support group meet say they thought they'd be labelled 'high maintenance', and that they felt extremely ashamed to tell the world that a second marriage had also failed. Society makes it tough with one divorce, but a second one makes it even harder to navigate. However, people like Anya sharing their story could help to chip away at this fear and hopefully also spread hope for other women finding themselves at the end of another marriage. If one divorce is normal, then every subsequent divorce is normal too!

When I started looking for stories of hope, I found them everywhere. Each story filled me with so much joy, love and hope. Yes, a divorce can really take a toll on a person. I've seen some who swore never to fall in love again only to find themselves swept off their feet a few years later. Many people who walk into court walk out feeling like it's the end. What we sometimes don't realize is that it's also a new beginning. You've walked into a life that is extremely different from your past, and you have no idea where to begin, much like when I started writing this book and found myself staring at a blank page on Word. Similarly, even if you do walk out of the court feeling like you've given up hope, I trust the stories you just read will give you renewed energy to write your own story of hope as you see fit. I know it worked for me.

Planning to Get Married?

A close friend's mother used to tell us that marriage is always a gamble. You have to take a chance and see how it goes. There are many of us who have been through the cycle of marriage and divorce at least once, so here's something I put together to make it easier for those who're thinking of getting married.

In hindsight, there are so many things a lot of us wish we'd done differently. This leaves us with lessons for the next time. It also makes us cautious as we cannot know what lies in store for the future. While speaking about this, so many women said 'if only someone had told me back then', which gave me the idea to pen down this chapter for you. Think of it as a pot of gold that could double up as that wise friend giving you solid, quality advice.

I hope that this is immensely helpful to you. Here's a crowdsourced list of advice from those who've been married or divorced, for those considering getting married.

- Be financially independent! These are the most essential words of advice. No matter how wonderful your partner might be, don't let yourself be dependent on anybody to take care of you. Ensure you have a flow of income and a bank account for your savings that's yours alone. Financial freedom empowers you to make major life decisions and support yourself and your child or children, if needed.

- Red flags won't just disappear as soon as you tie the knot. If there are issues that you're questioning, don't ignore them. Question the red flags, call for an intervention and then decide on the best course of action. It's the little things that build up to become a big monster later. If you find yourself brushing it off as something that will get fixed in the future, in all probability, it won't. Address it now. Don't get married until you know the red flags are being addressed. Ignoring red flags is the biggest mistake 90 per cent admit to and deeply regret.

- Your individuality matters. Marriage might change your life but it doesn't have to change you entirely. Keep a bit of yourself for you, always. All your personal interests cannot align with another person's. Continue to invest in yourself, and make time to enjoy the little things that make you, you.

- Love is important but trust and respect will take you a long way. You might find a comfortable rhythm with love but it's the trust you have for each other and the respect between the two of you, and socially, that will enable you to overcome hurdles and difficult situations. Because let's face it, every marriage will put you through some kind of test. A marriage can easily become turbulent without mutual respect.

- Don't confuse a wedding and a marriage. A wedding is only the beginning. Don't lose focus on the marriage by placing more importance on the wedding. Conversations about your life together will be far more important than anything that happens at a single-day event. Give more thought to your life than one day's celebration.

- Don't rush into a marriage. Take your time to understand the other person and put your compatibility to the test. Be as sure as you can before getting married. Think it through a thousand times at least.

- Don't fixate on age-based milestones. It's how you feel that matters. Choose a relationship because you want to be in it, and not because you've turned a certain age. If you're feeling pressured to get married, find the strength to resist. It'll lead to better decisions, and you'll feel better prepared for marriage at the right moment.

- There is no 'perfect' person. Everybody has shortcomings, including you. Keep that communication open by exposing your worst qualities, your flaws and your pet peeves, and seeing how the other reacts to them.

- In a lot of Indian families, parental interference is high. Speak to your partner about how much you are going to allow this type of interference inside your boundary, more so for women. Are you going to be living with your in-laws? That comes with different rules and flexibility (or lack of it). Talk about it before you get married.

- Do you want children, or not? It's extremely difficult to build a life together if you don't have clarity on this. If you do want children, speak in detail about how you'd want to raise them—religion, food habits, finances, belief systems, etc.

- Do you share the same political alignment? Do your values overlap?

- Past trauma can always catch up with you, be it from relationships, childhood or anything else. How would your partner deal with your triggers? Are you ready to deal with your partner's triggers? Don't ignore them. Talk it out. It might lead to a healthier relationship between the two of you.

- Looks will fade. Be realistic. You won't be the same shape or size. Neither will your partner. Don't base your relationship on looks. It's better to focus on your emotional compatibility.

- If you take romance out of the equation, are you really good friends? Are you able to discuss all the topics under the sun, have disagreements and learn from each other?

- Live together! (If you can)

- Understand, and take time to know yourself before investing in knowing another person. The better you know yourself, the more confident you will be. Your twenties might be best spent befriending yourself. Don't attach guilt to it. Rather, enjoy the process.

- Take time to speak about sexual intimacy. What do you like and what does your partner like?

- Women, don't change your name unless you really want to. It's an onerous task with documents to change your name. If you end up getting divorced, you will need to repeat the procedures to restore your maiden name.

- Ending a marriage is not a 'failure', so don't go into one with the intention of 'winning'. There is no winning or losing here.

- Patriarchy is going to be part of almost every household. Before you get married, discuss with your partner how you wish to deal with situations that might arise out of it.

- A marriage isn't just two people. It involves two families. Depending on your closeness to the family, have open conversations to ensure you set healthy boundaries, as far as possible. Their reaction to the boundaries you set might be a good way to assess your future family. Respect your partner and their family.

- Believe that you are full, capable and happy. Society has fed us this notion of a partner 'completing' us as the highest form of happiness. This is a highly romanticized concept of love created by movies. You cannot equate that to a marriage. Let a partner complement you, not complete you.

- Don't make a rash decision when you're younger. Give yourself time to grow up.

- Your freedom should be of utmost importance to you. If it feels like you're trading in freedom to be married, then it's probably time to re-evaluate your choices. Marriage should not feel like you're in jail.

- You'll be sharing a house with your partner (sometimes their family too). Discuss the distribution of domestic chores and how you intend to run the house together, as a team. It might sometimes feel like a small thing before marriage, but over time, it could become the biggest point of contention if the distribution isn't fair.

- If you're choosing to get married, you must speak about divorce as a concept as well, not with the intention of separating but to know that divorce is an option that exists and what the other feels about it. Check the stigma meter and use it as a filter to vet your partner.

- Travel together if you can, before tying the knot. You learn a lot about a person when you take a trip together.

- Have you seen your partner angry? Irritable? In a tough situation? Pissed off? Have you noticed how they behave in the spur of the moment?

- Try to spend quality time with your partner's friends as much as possible. It's a great way to understand someone's life journey and who they were before they met you.

- Are you both truly having fun together?

- If you're being forced into marriage, resist as much as possible. Ask for help from friends, family and those around you to gather support. If you're not happy, there are high chances of the marriage collapsing.

- Don't leave your dream job for a marriage if it means you lose your financial independence.

- You need a support system even on your best days. Maintain your close friendships. You always need support, on good days, and even more so on the bad days.

- If your gut says no, then it's a no. If your gut does not give you a clear signal, that's a no too. Believe it when it's a resounding yes from your gut. Ironically, it's far more reliable than your brain.

- Yes, divorce is common today. But don't let it deter you from getting married or scare you, if you think that's something you want to try. There is a lot of love in the world to receive and give. There are also so many marriages that leave one in awe. That could be yours. Don't lose heart. You'll learn for yourself. Everybody's journey is different. Live freely.

A Letter to My Twenty-Three-Year-Old Self

Dear Younger Me,

Take three steps back. You're fast, you're excited, and you're quick to trust everybody. While it might feel great at that moment, it can also lead to you making decisions you may regret later. You're only twenty-three. There's a lot left to live. You're freaking out about turning twenty-five? Ha! Wait for the calm and peace you'll feel when you're thirty.

I am you but I'm also not you. It's only been eight years since you were twenty-three, and you can't even imagine how much everything is going to change. Upside down.

Take three steps back. I don't want you to sit in front of a therapist one day and cry about how you wasted your twenties making bad decisions. I don't want you to feel like you're incapable of trusting your choices. I don't want you to walk around with so much weight from your past that it affects every part of your life in some way.

You're not a bad person.

You're kind and smart. The world doesn't know yet how strong you can be. Actually, you yourself don't know it yet. Strength doesn't mean you need to wake up a superhuman every day. There's a great deal of strength in vulnerability.

Take three steps back. I hope you remember that there's a lot of time left to prove yourself to the world and to please society. Resist. Resist the pressure to turn your life upside down.

Everything you feel in your gut is correct. Stop questioning it. Listen to yourself. You're not stupid. Okay, debatable. But trust yourself more. You're quite capable.

Take three steps back. There's no time or space in your life for regret. Think about every choice you make. Listen to those around you as well. You have great friends and a beautiful family. They're communicating in more than just words to you. Listen intently to them.

It's like that biscuit in the chai. If you hold it in for too long, it's going to form a soggy lump at the bottom of the cup. So don't prolong things unnecessarily. Enjoy that cup of chai without interruption.

Take three steps back from society. They'll call you 'career-oriented' as an insult. But stay calm when they do, for it's your career that will take you places. They'll say you're disrespecting society for speaking about topics that are taboo. Stay calm when they do, for you'll be helping more people than you imagined you would. They'll make you feel small, meek and helpless. Stay calm when they do, for they haven't seen your strength and determination as yet. They'll try to put you down, but they haven't seen you rise up yet.

It's okay. It's okay even if you don't take three steps back. Like I said, there is no space for regret in your life. All you need to know is that your thirty-one-year-old self is proud of you, for you're the nicest twenty-three-year-old she knows.

Love.

So, Wait, Is Divorce Really Normal?

Well, yes and no.

Divorce is still highly stigmatized in society, but the more common it gets, the more chances there are of the stigma reducing. India boasts of a 1–2 per cent divorce rate, which is nothing to boast about because it's not like we're surrounded by happy marriages. The truth is that we don't have the infrastructure or the support to help those in unhappy marriages. The solution to this is for more support groups to be formed, to create safe and happy spaces for people to thrive, accept that marriage is a choice and be kinder to those who want to opt out of it. It's also equally important for every family to understand that if their son or daughter is getting married, then there's a possibility it will end in divorce.

I've been accused of 'glorifying' divorce by constantly speaking about it. I'm really not. My efforts have been to show the world that divorce is merely a choice—one that should be made keeping in mind that it could be the best decision individually, as well as for the couple. I'm expanding the canvas for divorce to be more widely accepted. Like many other life choices, let's accept the decision in that moment and then move on. It isn't the end of the world for the people getting divorced. Neither does this choice need to bring shame upon any family.

It actually all starts with the word itself. The reactions when you hear the word divorce need to be changed.

Like I'd mentioned earlier, the onus of detaching stigma from divorce doesn't need to stem only from those who've been divorced. Each one of us can make a difference, because it isn't something that's uncommon. We have married couples all around us, and when marriage is in the mix, divorce cannot be out of question. Whether you're divorced, married, single, committed or whatever else your relationship status might be, here's how you can contribute towards eliminating stigma in our country and society at large.

Speak up: We all know that one uncle or aunty at every function who ends up saying something unnecessary about divorce, if it comes up in a conversation. Don't laugh it off. Whenever you get the chance, educate people. Are you able to have more evolved discussions about divorce? It needn't be a heated argument. It can be two minutes of your time to tell someone not to make it worse.

It begins at home: How do your parents and immediate family react to divorce? Have a conversation with them and understand what they feel, regardless of your marital status. Ask them how they'd react if you were to have a divorce, and encourage them to understand their own feelings first, even if it's uncomfortable at that moment. There is so much opportunity to grow from discomfort.

Check in with others: We all know someone who is in an unhappy marriage. Look around you. Check in, when your bandwidth allows, to see how they're doing. You never know who might want to read that text from you, that very moment. If you have a friend or relative going through a tough time, see how you can help them. Let them know they're not alone.

Don't force: You cannot force someone into getting divorced. It needs to come from them. Instead, sit with them, offer comfort and listen to them. In most cases, people just want to be heard and validated.

Check in with yourself: What's your stigma meter? Have you gotten over the stigma of divorce? Most times, stigma is heavily internalized by the impact of what we've heard and learnt growing up, and that's okay. But are you cognizant of it? Have conversations with yourself to see how you feel about it. If you feel comfortable, speak to your friends about it too.

Support: We all pick our own battles, so go ahead and choose what you deeply feel for. But if you wish to help this cause, it doesn't take much to support others like me who are talking about normalizing divorce and shattering the stigma around it. Trust me, even one share on social media propels our cause forward.

We might have a long way to go in terms of normalizing divorce in every household. But I know for sure that we're making progress and taking a step in the right direction. Even me writing this book is one such step. Reading a book on this topic is another step.

Open conversations, sharing opinions and real experiences, support groups, less judgement and more love can lead to a campaign like #DivorceIsNormal becoming obsolete. Because one day, I believe it will be so normal that kids won't even comprehend why this hashtag was relevant. That's the aim—to help it reach every household's dinner conversation, to help parents welcoming their children back home so they are safe, to not worrying about what others will say, to not raising eyebrows when someone is getting divorced, to not expecting parents to stick together for the sake of their children, and to being there for each other through good times and bad.

Like all social justice fights, we can only build it step by step, together.

So, shall we start?